MOVEMENT ACTIVITY
IN GYMNASTICS

MOVEMENT ACTIVITY IN GYMNASTICS

by

Jennifer K. Holbrook

*Principal Lecturer and Head of the Women's
Department of Physical Education,
The College of Education, Bognor Regis*

Publishers   PLAYS, INC.   Boston

©

MACDONALD AND EVANS LIMITED
1973

This book is copyright and may not be reproduced in
whole or in part (except for purposes of review) without
the express permission of the publishers in writing

First American edition published by Plays, Inc.
1974

Published in Great Britain under the title,
Gymnastics: A Movement Activity

Library of Congress Cataloging in Publication Data

Holbrook, Jennifer K.
    Movement activity in gymnastics.

    "Published in Great Britain under the title:
Gymnastics: a movement activity."
    1. Gymnastics for children.   2. Movement
notation. I. Title.
GV464.5.H64   1974   372.8'6   73-13928
ISBN 0-8238-0158-6

Printed in Great Britain

Preface

In writing this book, my main intention has been to give some help to all those teachers and students who recognise the need of young children to come to terms with their physical environment, who appreciate children's enjoyment of activities such as hanging, leaping, sliding, swinging and balancing and who wish to know how to develop this natural appetite for moving in an acrobatic way on apparatus.

While the movement material in the text is derived from the principles of movement expounded by Rudolf Laban, I have deliberately made a certain selection and simplification. This is in part necessary since the material is selected for work with children aged from five to eleven years, but also because of the essential character of gymnastic work, which is concerned with practical "doing" and not "dancing." Although both activities may share similar movement ideas, the underlying intention is fundamentally different. In gymnastics, the concern is to explore and invent movement sequences where the focus is on handling oneself in relation to specialised apparatus while experiencing the joy of playing with gravity and exploring problems of balance. In creative dance, the emphasis is on the forming of movement ideas in an artistic way to communicate moods, thoughts and feelings.

Part One is designed to help teachers identify the core content of movement, since all too often teachers are prevented from developing the children's movement activity through lack of basic movement knowledge.

Certain themes with which teachers may be familiar from other texts have been omitted, for example, the theme of weight transference, since I feel this has caused some confusion and there is a misplaced emphasis on what is bound to occur. Unless a child is to stay rooted to the spot, weight transference, which has been variously described as travelling or linking movements, must take place. The challenge is to enable children to discover and identify, for example, what actions will result from moving on to different parts of the body as they travel on, off and over the apparatus.

The whole emphasis in Part One is placed on developing children's feel for such factors as the different actions that the body can do, the way in which energy can be varied in different activities, where the movement can go in space, the relatedness of one part of the body to another and the ability to explore movement ideas with a partner.

A vocabulary of words, by no means exhaustive, is included, since a wide vocabulary is essential if a teacher is to develop an articulate approach to the different components of movement involved in a child's attempts to create a movement phrase.

Part Two considers the teaching problems, with guidelines on lesson planning, observation and evaluation of movement. The lesson outlines are designed to illustrate the way in which movement material can be developed in the lesson situation, but they are simply one interpretation using material based on ideas which have been found helpful to teachers and students beginning in this field.

It is my hope that this book will enable some teachers to begin, others to continue, and perhaps experienced teachers to gain further stimulus, in what can prove a fascinating and enjoyable area of the Movement Education programme.

April 1973   J.K.H.

Acknowledgments

THERE are many sources to which I am indebted in the development of my thinking on the subject of gymnastics. There are the children and students it has been my privilege to work with and the stimulation given by former teachers and colleagues, in particular, arising from my study at the Art of Movement Studio, whose Director was then Miss Lisa Ullman.

Especial thanks go to the Headmaster and staff of the Captain John Palliser School and the University Elementary School, Calgary, for their co-operation in providing classes and their willingness to try out the lesson outlines; to Ray Crawford, who first read the raw material and gave encouragement when I was working at the University of Calgary; to Barbara Smith, Senior Tutor at Bognor Regis College of Education, and Hilary Corlett, Principal Lecturer at Chelsea College of Physical Education, who generously gave of their time in reading and discussing the text from the non-specialist and specialist viewpoint; to Margaret Slowman, Principal Lecturer at Didsbury College of Education, who worked so willingly with the children, and to her husband John, whose enthusiasm and photographic skill captured the children in action. Finally, I shall always be grateful to Dr. Lew Goodwin, Director of the School of Physical Education, University of Calgary, who gave me the opportunity to lecture in Canada; it was during this time that I began to write down my first thoughts for this book.

Contents

CONTENTS

List of Illustrations

Part One

The Core Content of Movement

CHAPTER I

Historical Perspective

Introduction

As an ingredient of Physical Education, gymnastics has undergone many changes; these in turn have reflected attitudes towards the education of children, from the instrumental model to the child-centred idea. The very change in terminology—"Physical Training" has become "Physical Education" or even "Movement Education," and "Gymnastics" has become "Educational Gymnastics"—signifies not only growth and development of ideas about "what" gymnastics is about but also "how" it should be taught.

The Swedish system of gymnastics reflected an era when the emphasis was placed on instructing children, with an imposed discipline and consequently a formal relationship between teacher and taught. While this undoubtedly aided the less competent teacher, it implied a way of teaching and a type of lesson which suited every class and every child. The basis of the work was anatomical, with a certain remedial emphasis, concerned with the systematic training of muscles and joints in addition to developing strength, endurance and a quick response to command. There was an inevitable limitation of the range of movement possibilities, much of the work being symmetric, planal and rhythmically limited. The uniqueness of the individual was largely unrecognised or ignored.

Changes in Approach

In the late 1930s, certain major changes in the education of young children (age range five–eleven years) were already being implemented, as a result of work in the field of educational psychology and child development by Freud, Dewey, Piaget and Cyril Burt. Primary school teachers were quick to recognise the importance of providing an environment which enabled the young child to explore and experiment, and consequently develop, areas of knowledge and new skills. Activity became the key word, as teachers concerned themselves with providing a stimulating environment in which the different facets of the whole person—physical, intellectual, emotional and social—could be brought into play.

The *Hadow Report*[1] was a positive catalyst for physical educationists, since the implications of the Report could not be disregarded. The limitations of the Swedish system had been increasingly recognised, and there was a growing appreciation of the need for work which was more meaningful to children, and which involved more than the mere acquisition of skills.

Throughout history, wars and rumours of wars have been responsible for precipitating changes and causing chance relationships which ultimately have far-reaching effects; this has been the case not least in the field of education. The Second World War and the years 1940–1945 revealed two sources which were instrumental in bringing about radical changes in the content of, and the approach to, gymnastic work. The Army, with new methods of training for commando work, proved a source of inspiration for the development of new apparatus designed to satisfy the needs of children to hang, climb, swing and balance. Children in the primary schools were encouraged to work at their own level and explore the possibilities of the new apparatus.

The second, and decisive, influence for change came largely through the recognition of the work of Rudolf Laban, whose arrival in England prior to the outbreak of war has been termed by some an "historical accident."[2]

Women physical educationists were the first to recognise the importance and value of Laban's concept of human movement in which the motion factors of Time, Weight, Space and Flow were conceived as the common denominators.

Lisa Ullmann and others who pioneered Laban's work in dance in education, and Ruth Morison who took the lead in the field of gymnastics, opened the way for new lesson material concerned with "thinking and feeling in terms of movement," which recognised the creative and inventive powers of children by its teaching approach. Both dance and gymnastic work was initially distinguished by the prefix "Modern Educational" to avoid confusion with other forms then existing within the schools, although for some teachers there was even disagreement as to whether gymnastics was a "movement" or an "agility" lesson.

As with many innovations, some mistakes were made in the development of new ideas, largely through a misunderstanding of basic principles. Men physical educationists and not a few women were strongly critical of the

4

"new" gymnastics. In part, this was not surprising, since it demanded a complete reappraisal of the basis of their work and of the teacher–child relationship. In addition, many were still concerned with evaluating work in terms of common standards and with the effects of mobility, strength and endurance. The fact that a purposeful programme could still achieve anatomical and physiological benefits as natural outcomes was unrecognised.[3] However, the value of the new work being implemented in the schools was given due recognition in the Ministry of Education publication *Moving and Growing*, in 1952, and the latest publication by the D.E.S.—*Movement—Physical Education in the Primary School*, 1972, strengthens the case for this approach.

While physical educationists in England had been seeking new ideas, it should not be forgotten that as far back as 1924 pioneers in North America such as Jesse F. Williams, M.D., had recognised that children have a natural interest in activities which involve climbing, hanging and leaping and had presented "a new view of physical education based upon the biologic unity of mind and body."[4] Dr. Jay B. Nash, Head of the Department of Physical Education at New York University had also been concerned with pioneering programmes based on natural movement which recognised the organic unity of the individual.

However, while the world of dance education flourished under the enlightened leadership of such educators as Margaret H'Doubler and Ruth Murray, who recognised the need for creativity and the implications for learning movement skills, the same could not be said in the development of gymnastic work. Gymnastics continued to develop along more formal lines and the emphasis remained on set movement patterns designed to develop strength, agility, endurance and balance. This was particularly true of the 1950s, when physical fitness became a national concern. In addition, interest in success at Olympic level was a determining factor in the growth of this in school and college programmes. It is only through the development of jet-age travel and mass media communications that the exchange of ideas at international level has led to the movement approach to gymnastics being increasingly recognised in the U.S.A. and Canada, and other Commonwealth countries. "The sense of adventure, daring, creativity and an ability to handle themselves on large apparatus impressed me as I watched the five-to-seven-year-olds;" "the major contribution to learning is that movement education tends to develop a

5

positive self-concept."[5] These were two comments from participants in the second Anglo-American workshop on Movement Education.

While a movement approach may still be new to many teachers working abroad, the majority of teachers in Britain have been familiar with this way of working for over twenty years. (This does not mean, however, that there is necessarily general satisfaction with the overall development of the work.) By allowing scope for inventiveness, involving the child not only in doing, but in thinking and feeling, which previous traditional forms of gymnastics failed to do, a child comes to understand the nature of gymnastic activity in a meaningful way through a heightened awareness of the component elements of movement.

REFERENCES

1. *Report of the Consultative Committee on the Primary School*, H.M.S.O., 1931.
2. Jean Carroll and Peter Lofthouse, *Creative Dance for Boys*, Macdonald and Evans, Ltd., 1969, p. 5.
3. More recently recognised in a paper by B. Davies in the *British Journal of Physical Education*, Vol. 2, No. 4, July 1971.
4. *Journal of Higher Education*, May 1930.
5. *J.O.H.P.E.R.*, January 1967.

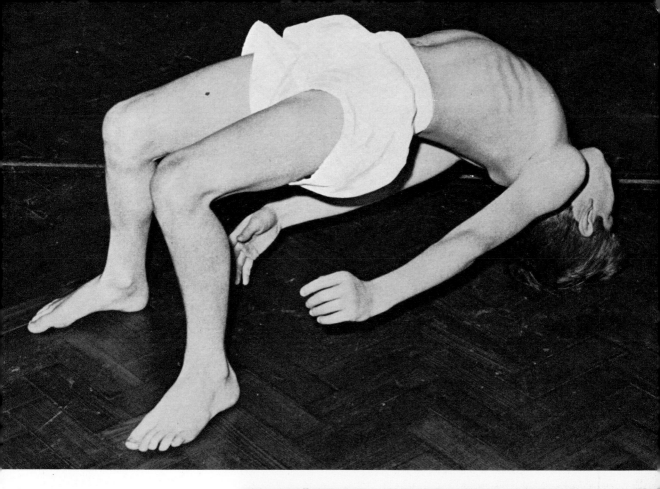

PLATE 1—ABOVE

Arching while balancing on head and feet.

PLATE 2—RIGHT

Momentary contact while working on a partner task of matching shapes.

PLATE 3
An eight-year-old mastering a spread shape while jumping.

CHAPTER II

The Material of Movement

Introduction

YOUNG children bring to the school situation a tremendous capacity for a variety of movement, and a considerable mastery of it, evidenced in their love of such actions as jumping, climbing, hanging, swinging and sometimes spinning around, for no particular reason except that of sheer enjoyment of the movement sensation. There is, therefore, a natural source of movement material for the teacher to develop in various ways.

The provision of apparatus, whether in a multi-purpose hall or in a specially constructed gymnasium, can contribute towards an environment where a child's innate desire to play with and defy gravity, to explore spaces which can be moved through, and to experiment with ways of moving on, along, off, over and around obstacles can be satisfied.

As teachers, it is our task to harness this natural potential in such a way that the child ". . . is initiated into the content of the activity or forms of knowledge in a meaningful way, so that he knows what he is doing."[1] This pre-supposes relevant knowledge and understanding—of children and how they learn, of their needs, capacities and capabilities and, not least, of movement material.

Since we are primarily concerned with *children in action* and with movement understanding, what matters subsequently is developing a conscious awareness of WHAT one is doing, HOW one is moving, WHERE one moves and WITH WHAT RELATIONSHIP one moves through, pinpointing a particular aspect of movement in a meaningful way.

The material for developing children's movement potential can be divided into four main aspects:

1. THE BODY IN ACTION —What moves.

2. THE MOTION FACTORS—How one moves.

3. SPACE AWARENESS   —Where one moves.

4. RELATIONSHIPS   —With what relationship one moves.

The Body in Action

Exploring the body's potential for movement, developing the feel not only for the whole body in motion but also for the relationship of the various parts to the whole, and what these parts can do, is important in reawakening the kinesthetic sense and developing a feel for co-ordinated movement.

Focus on the basic movements of bend, stretch and twist—movements which are bound to occur in action to a greater or lesser degree—has, in the past, led to a good deal of static work. The emphasis must be on the bodily change which occurs as the children are rounding, stretching, arching and twisting in a variety of actions.

Basic Movements

1. ROUNDING OR CURLING

Curling: This movement occurs when the spine is rounded and the extremities are brought towards each other, the whole body curling and becoming more compact, for example, when rolling in a ball-like way or when curling around a bar in a forwards direction. Ideas such as bringing the head and shoulders towards the hips and the feet towards the hands, tucking in the sharp points of elbows and knees, can enhance the feel for this movement when balancing, travelling or jumping. Again, the curving of the spine is important in rocking actions.

Arching: Children can also discover that they can curl their spines and surround the space at their sides, and that when the spine and limbs extend not only away from the centre but into the space behind, arching occurs. Experimenting with arching while balancing or travelling, *e.g.* when supported on hands and feet only, or achieving the feel for arching in elevation, can help produce some lively work while ensuring that movements which contribute to the children's natural mobility are maintained (*see* Plate 1).

2. TWISTING

A conscious awareness of the feel for twisting can occur when children explore the idea of fixing one part of the body, which may act as a point of support, and screwing the rest of the body away from and around it (*see* Plate 4). They may experience twisting when the top half of the body

8

continues to turn after the lower half, for example, has ceased to turn. They may also discover that twisting can lead them into a change of situation, for example, of level, or into balance on another part of the body. Nine- and ten-year-olds can explore the possibilities of twisting in the air through the idea of making hips and knees go in different directions as they jump, or different parts of the body, *e.g.* head, chest or arms, leading them into twisting in different forms of locomotion.

3. STRETCHING

In the children's day-to-day activities, the experience of fully stretching the extremities away from the centre of the body does not normally occur. Ideas such as stretch, pull out and extend as they jump and travel should enable the children to appreciate the difference between this body movement and that of curling or twisting. The children readily appreciate the "spoke-like" character of the movement and they may discover that they are basically flat, narrow or wide. When stretching, ankles, knees and finger-tips are often neglected, and attention should be drawn to them.

With all these movements (*see* Figure 1), the children can become aware that one may serve as a preparation for another. For example, stretching in order to curl around a bar, twisting in order to recoil into another twisting movement around a rope, or curling in preparation for arching.

A feel for the way in which motion travels from one part of the spine to another, together with an awareness of the head as an extension of the spine, is fundamental when developing these basic movements. As children begin to spend a greater part of their school day in a more sedentary way, combinations of curling, stretching and twisting in a variety of bodily actions can prove valuable in waking up the body, while incidentally strengthening and maintaining the natural mobility and suppleness of the spine.

Basic Activities

Children will naturally use a variety of bodily actions, and these may be grouped to reflect the roles that the limbs and trunk play in movement (*see* Figure 2).

I. STEPPING

This involves transferring the body weight using the normal points of support, *i.e.* the feet. Stepping is generally seen as a preparation for a main action and children should be encouraged to feel how the different parts of the feet contribute to a smooth and resilient preparation. In gymnastics,

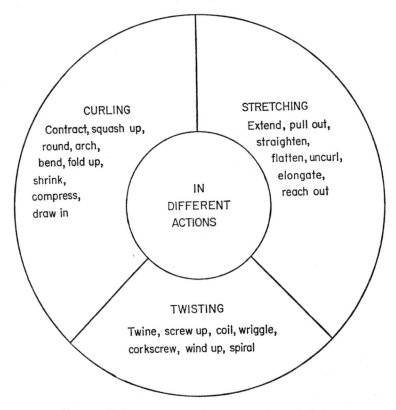

FIG. I.—Basic movements: the movement vocabulary.

children discover that it is possible to step on to other parts of the body (*e.g.*, knees, hands), but this definition is used to distinguish the normal from the unusual.

2. JUMPING

A fundamental means of "arriving on" or "departing from" apparatus is through jumping. It can be defined as a movement where the body leaves the floor or apparatus and is momentarily unsupported (*see* Plates 3, 5 and 9).

10

Young children enjoy this vital activity, as they attempt to defy gravity, often using the "two feet to two feet" jump, since this gives them a more stable base in preparation and recovery. Initially, there will be little real

STILLNESS

Balance, pause, stop, grip, freeze, static, hold, suspend, rest, stand, motionless

STEPPING

Walk, stride, skim, tiptoe, pace

TURNING

Revolve, spin, pivot, rotate, twirl, whirl, whizz round, gyrate, circle, spiral

ACTIVITIES CAN BE

on, off, over, around, through, along, under, Apparatus

LOCOMOTION

Roll, slide, rock, dive, slither, tumble, climb, cartwheel, crawl, "crab"

JUMPING

Hop, leap, fly, jig, pounce, spring, skip, bounce, run, gallop, bound

GESTURE

Close, contract, stretch, spread, swing, tip, tilt, rise, lift away

FIG. 2.—Basic activities: the movement vocabulary.

feel for elevation, their enjoyment coming from the sensation of dropping and from the feel of their feet hitting the floor.

Five Basic Jumps: The basic jumps can be summarised as from one foot to the same foot; from one foot to two feet; from two feet to one foot; from two feet to two feet and from one foot to the other.

The possible combinations of these basic jumps are numerous, and children can derive much pleasure from inventing their own jumping patterns. Developing a feel for bouncing and discovering and practising combinations of the five basic jumps when working in one place or when travelling, provides a further challenge to the children's skill and inventiveness whether in floorwork or on apparatus.

It should be recognised that repeated jumping can become tiring, the necessary vitality consequently being lost. Phrasing movement, alternating jumping with stillness or contrasting jumping with a different kind of action can help the children "re-charge their batteries" and serve as both a preparation and a recovery.

Pouncing and Springing: Perhaps it should be noted here that another kind of action which is very much characteristic of, and integral to, gymnastic work, might also be included under jumping. Pouncing or springing actions are fun to do and make parts of the body other than the feet receive and absorb the body weight after the moment of flight. A catspring is a typical example, but children can discover other springing and bouncing possibilities through experimenting with different starting situations.

Elevation: As children become more skilful, their mastery of jumping may be further challenged when they develop a feel for elevation through experiencing a momentary sensation of being suspended in the air. Words such as "buoyant," "airborne" and "suspended," together with an awareness of changing tensions and speed changes (*see* Chapter III), can help to develop their feel for elevation. Focus on the upper part of the body, particularly the head and chest—their centre of buoyancy—is fundamental when developing children's mastery of this vital activity. (This centre of buoyancy is sometimes referred to as "the centre of levity," a term invented by Laban to give active guidance in elevation.)

Ways of Landing: The ability to meet the floor in different ways is basic to the development of movement mastery. With young children, the easiest landing is coming down close to the floor and giving in to the force of gravity. Tucking the vulnerable parts of the body in and taking the weight on the broad surfaces of the body, as in rolling actions, is often a useful beginning and a safety factor. More challenging is to find different actions which they can do as they come down and regain contact with the floor or apparatus. A further progression is to come down and immediately thrust away again from the floor or apparatus. The whole focus is on coming down in order to jump again, using their energy to react in a spark-like way as soon as their feet make contact with the floor. The third possibility— of coming down and meeting the floor or apparatus, stabilising motion while retaining a sense of buoyancy and lightness—is the most challenging of all, and demands a sensitivity and vitality throughout the whole body.

3. LOCOMOTION

Synonymous with the idea of travelling, the word locomotion is used here to distinguish those forms of movement where parts of the body other than the normal, *i.e.* the feet, are involved in travelling, the emphasis being on moving from one place to another.

Typical gymnastic actions such as rolls, handstands and cartwheels (*see* Plates 7 and 16) will emerge, which are part of our gymnastic heritage, but, when the idea of travelling is linked with awareness of different parts of the body, children will discover many more action possibilities.

4. TURNING

Experience of movement which is rather more free-flowing and exhilarating to perform is enhanced through turning. Ideas such as pivoting, spinning, going around and revolving, involve the whole body in action and a change of front results. Discovering whole and half-turns can help children cultivate a sense for precision in space when moving to face in a new direction.

Awareness of new movement possibilities can arise through linking the idea of turning with different activities—jumping and turning, taking weight on hands and feet only and turning while travelling, or turning while travelling along a straight pathway. Children may discover that, while they can turn without twisting, they cannot twist without turning!

5. GESTURE

This can be defined as a movement of any part of the body which does not involve supporting the body weight. Children can experiment with ways in which a part of the body which is "free" in space may be used to assist in balance, initiate action or assist in building up momentum, for example, the legs can be used to lever the body into an inverted position or swing and whip the body off a point of balance.

Stillness and Balance

Stopping, gripping and pausing are all words which relate to moments of stillness, the cessation of visible motion. Sensitivity to stillness as an "active" movement, rather than one of giving up or collapse, is vital in

13

the forming of intelligible movement sentences. Appreciation of the right amount of tension to establish and maintain stillness or to release the body into motion helps children to become aware of the part that stillness plays in re-charging their "energy batteries." Recognition of stillness as a moment of preparation and or recovery, which may be of longer or shorter duration, will help children to establish a sense for rhythmical movement and to appreciate its contribution to the rhythm of action.

Children can discover the different ways of stopping—"putting the brakes on"—whether through a gradual slowing down or through a sudden increase in tension and gripping. They can be encouraged to choose their own actions and to select their own moments of balancing (see Plate 8) and pausing or gripping and putting a "full stop" at the end of their movement sentence.

In relation to stillness, children can become aware that movement may begin and end in any one of four basic situations, that is, standing, sitting, kneeling and lying, according to the movement idea being worked upon. Perhaps more important, the children appreciate that this stillness and balance is often a moment when they are inverted. The world is "upside down," and this contributes to the movement character of gymnastic work.

The ability to link one action to another, and one activity with another, is fundamental to the invention of simple movement phrases. A feel for movement "logic," an ability to sense the way in which one action relates to the next, is vital if children are to develop continuity and fluency of movement.

The Alphabet of the Body

Young children may have a considerable vocabulary of actions involving the whole body but, while aware of hands and feet, they may not have a differentiated awareness of what these parts can do or the way in which they contribute to a skilful movement. By focussing attention on parts of the body in motion and stillness, a more articulate use of the body may be developed.

I. CONTACT WITH THE FLOOR

Step-like Actions: Children can discover that different parts of the body *e.g.* hands, knees, shoulders, hips, can receive the weight of the body as they travel, and that by keeping one part of the body always in contact with the floor or apparatus, they can make "*step-like*" actions. They can experiment with stepping on to these different parts of the body in succession, becoming aware of the chosen part leading the way, being moved over or balanced on.

2. USING BROAD SURFACES

Sliding, Rolling, Rocking: The broad surfaces of the body can be moved on to produce sliding actions, and with continuous change from one surface to another, rolling actions will result (*see* Plate 19). By taking the idea of "to and fro" in relation to the chosen surfaces, the children can develop rocking actions (*see* Plate 10). Awareness of the rounding and arching of the spine is fundamental here, since a flat back with an unyielding spine can cause jolting and bruising.

3. STRESSING BODY PARTS IN THE AIR

Different parts of the body may be stressed in the air when jumping or may be used to initiate action; for example, the hips can move away from the point of support and send the body into motion.

4. GRIPPING

Different parts of the body can be used for gripping when working on apparatus, *e.g.* hips and knees can grip on bars or ropes.

5. SUPPORT AND BALANCE

Many parts of the body can provide support as a point of balance. Children can discover interesting balances through relating parts of the body to balance on with ideas such as matching or contrasting parts. Selecting parts to balance on from one side of the body only, *e.g.* left knee and hand, as opposed to both hands, can considerably exercise their control as well as prove a challenge to their inventiveness. Children very quickly discover that the broad surfaces are more helpful to balance on but find it challenging to use the small areas of the body such as head, hands and knees.

Body Shape

As a result of the particular structure of the human body, and the basic movements of which the body is capable, four basic shapes may be created in motion and stillness.

1. LONG AND NARROW

This shape (*see* Plates 7 and 13) stresses the length of the body—the long line of the spine—and develops an awareness of the head, upper and lower limbs extending away from the centre into the space above and below the body. There is a single-dimensional feel to the movement, and it can be achieved when jumping, rolling or balancing.

2. BROAD AND SPREADING

The width of the body can be stressed when the upper and lower limbs stretch and extend away from each other into the space at the sides (*see* Plate 3). This wide shape gives a two-dimensional feel to movement, as can be seen in star jumps and cartwheels, and can be achieved in other forms of locomotion, in addition to stillness.

3. ROUND AND BALL-LIKE

This shape is formed when the ends of the body meet or converge and the spine arches or curls. Generally achieved in rolling actions, this shape may also be experienced in other forms of locomotion, for example, in rocking actions, and while not helpful to elevation, there will always be some children who will produce it in jumping (*see* Plate 5).

4. SCREW-LIKE AND TWISTED

A twisting movement can lead to the forming of a twisted shape, one part of the body acting against another and giving a three-dimensional feel. When experimenting with this shape on apparatus, it is helpful to provide apparatus with a narrow surface which the body can twist around, for example, ropes, bars and climbing frames (*see* Plate 4).

Children can experiment with finding shapes they can achieve in stillness and balance, retaining a shape as they travel within a series of different actions or changing from one shape to another in different forms of motion. Emphasis on shape can give children a sense for clarity of bodily action, but care is needed in teaching to avoid children producing a series of positions. The emphasis should be on *change* from one shape to another in motion, for example, "Can you make a shape in the air, then land and change shape as you travel along the mat?"

Symmetry and Asymmetry

While the human body has a natural right-left symmetry, it is usual to move and perform many tasks using one side more actively than the other, according to whether a person is right- or left-handed.

I. SYMMETRY

Children may develop a conscious awareness of the feel of symmetry through such tasks as "Make both sides do the same in the air," or "Use hands and feet only as you travel and make both sides do the same thing at the same time." They may discover that such actions have a very even feel, that symmetry allows movement only in the dimensional directions of up, down, forwards and backwards, involves only stretching, rounding or arching, and is helpful to balance and stillness. Later, they may discover that the only floor pattern that is possible is along a line.

2. ASYMMETRY

On the other hand, through exploring the feel of asymmetry in different activities, children can appreciate that turning and twisting become involved and that consequently there is a possibility of greater variety of bodily action and increased directional possibilities. Children may discover that asymmetry is helpful in stressing the "going" in movement, and enjoy the sensation of "off balance" that asymmetry gives (*see* Plate 11).

Asymmetry may be experienced through such challenges as "Can you take both legs to the same side in the air?" or "Find a point of balance then tip off to one side." Children should be encouraged to explore ways of moving with not only one side being more active but also with both sides doing the same, and to experience the change from one to another within the same or a series of different actions.

Summary of Material

Awareness of WHAT the body is doing (*see* Figure 3) grows from:

1. Experience of the basic movements.
2. Awareness of the whole body in motion and stillness.
3. Knowledge of what parts of the body can do in touching, gripping, supporting, leading, receiving weight and initiating action.

17

4. The sense of the changing shape of the body in the basic activities.

5. Emphasis on symmetry and asymmetry.

The awakening of the kinesthetic sense through focus on what the body is doing in action should help children to become increasingly skilful in

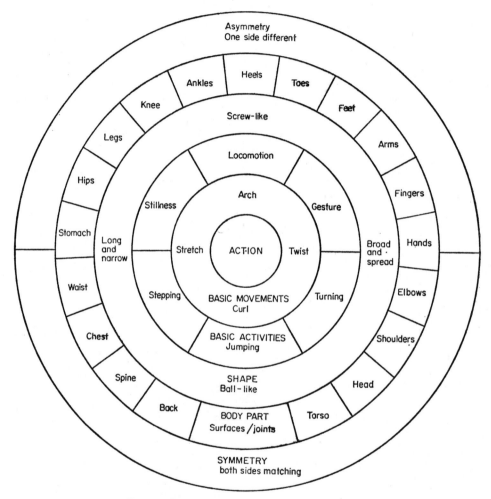

FIG. 3.—Summary of movements and activities.

their body management. A growing comprehension of the WHAT of movement will help to increase the children's movement resources and enable them to formulate sentences of action in a coherent and logical manner.

REFERENCES

1. R. S. Peters, *Education as Initiation*, an inaugural lecture delivered at the University of London Institute of Education, December 1963, published by C. Harrap & Co., Ltd., 1964.

CHAPTER III

The Dynamics of Movement

CHAPTER II was concerned with directing children's attention to what the body was doing in action: knowing *what part, what shape, what activity.* Through the flow of one movement to the next, the children will have moved with varying degrees of muscular energy or FORCE, and their actions will have taken a certain span of TIME as they evolved in SPACE.

The children's efforts (*see* Figure 4) will have revealed not only their assessment of the kind of energy required to answer a movement problem, but also something which is characteristic both of the group and of individual children: it cannot be denied that a child may experience a sense of drama at being able to hang upside down from a climbing frame (*see* Plate 15), or may express delight when leaping from a box. As Margarete Streicher aptly states, "in every voluntary movement the personal form of expression is to be seen."[1]

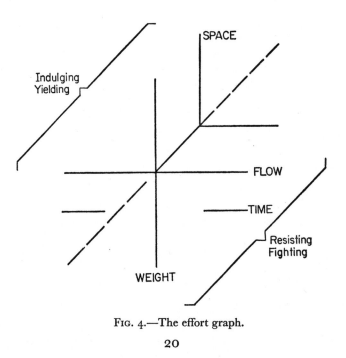

FIG. 4.—The effort graph.

However, in a movement situation concerned with objective "doing" and not "dancing," it is to the practical aspect of these factors that attention should be directed. The very fact that considerations of strength and choice of speed inevitably occur when children are faced with moving on apparatus

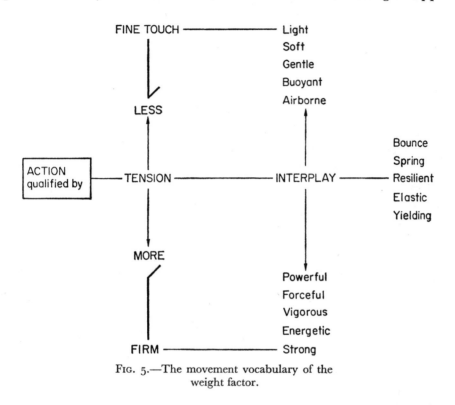

FIG. 5.—The movement vocabulary of the weight factor.

and that they may experience difficulty, not only in selecting the appropriate energy to arrive on the apparatus but also in making transitions from one activity to the next, indicates that there is a need to focus on the Effort content of movement.[2]

In developing awareness of HOW one moves, it is important to understand that the Motion Factors are not "applied" to gymnastic work, but the reverse, the efforts already inherent in movement being highlighted where appropriate.

The Weight Factor

Everyday activities demand that we handle the physical weight of our body in motion and stillness and, in addition, select the appropriate muscular tension when handling and manipulating objects (*see* Figure 5). Fluctuations in our energy may be revealed through movements which have a vigorous energetic and purposeful expression, in contrast to movements which are lighter and more delicate. Thus there is a constant adjustment in the use of muscular energy, varying from powerful, strong and firm to weak and light—consciously or unconsciously.

1. CHANGING TENSIONS

Through action and stillness, children can discover the changing tensions of the body, becoming more aware of the muscular feel of movement. Children may discover the strong tension needed to thrust the body away from the floor in jumping and the sensitive tension needed through the legs as they meet the floor for lightness in landing. They may become aware of how much tension is needed in the body to maintain a point of balance and experiment with different ways of using their energy in order to leave it. Is it through an increase of tension—a thrust away from their point of balance? Is it through a gradual release of tension—a controlled movement away from their point of balance?

Children enjoy playing with changing tensions and quickly realise that inappropriate tension can hinder continuity and ease of movement. For example, too much tension, especially in the shoulders, can hinder their sense for elevation and in the lower limbs can cause hardness and jarring in their landings. Equally, too little tension, particularly in the legs and in the trunk leads to a bodily slackness which makes the establishment of inverted balances difficult and contributes to a loss of control.

2. QUALITATIVE ASPECTS

The contrast between the extreme possibilities of the weight factor, producing a qualitative feel for movement involving not only action but sensation, gives added liveliness to the children's movement. Firmness can be experienced in thrusting away from a point of balance, in pulling actions along a bench, in whipping turning jumps on the ropes or in strong levering actions to establish an inverted balance. The contrasting quality of fine touch can be experienced in lightly running, leaping and landing softly, in lifting lightly away from a point of balance and in experiencing

22

PLATE 4—ABOVE

Work on twisting.

PLATE 5—BELOW LEFT

An eight-year-old mastering a tucked
shape while jumping.

PLATE 6—BELOW RIGHT

From feet to hands then hips.

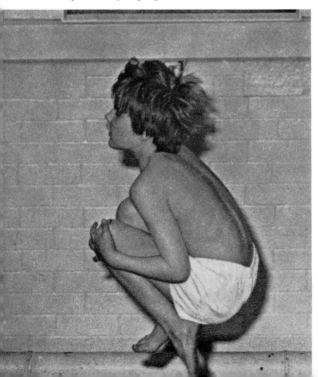

PLATE 7—LEFT
Part of a gymnastic heritage—a handstand
with a real feel for extension.

PLATE 8—BELOW
Balancing in different ways.

a moment of suspension or in meeting the floor gently with different surfaces and parts of the body.

Experimenting with different amounts of muscular tension in a variety of bodily actions and stillness contributes to a growing awareness of the need for the appropriate tension in relation to the task and the realisation that "the extremes of strong and weak tensions are necessary . . . but they are useless without the smooth transition from one to the other to achieve a resilient fluency of movement."[3]

The Time Factor

As children move, they may discover that accompanying the increase or decrease in tension there is a change in the speed of their actions (*see* Figure 6). Exploring the possibility of TIME changes can considerably enlarge the children's movement experience and give to their work the necessary vitality and rhythmical awareness. As with other movement ideas, contrast—in this instance, of speed—is more easily accomplished before developing a feel for a gradual change of effort.

I. QUANTITATIVE ASPECTS: QUICK/SLOW

Children can discover actions where they can move QUICKLY and maintain the same speed, *e.g.* rolls, a series of quick jumps or pouncing actions.

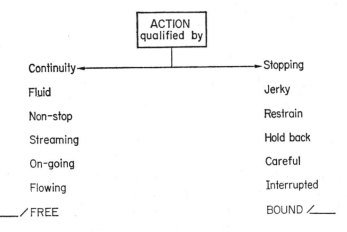

Fig. 6.—The movement vocabulary of the time factor.

THE DYNAMICS OF MOVEMENT

They might be asked to select one action, repeat it three or four times, then pause, the pause acting as a moment of recovery. The children might then be asked to explore different ways of moving SLOWLY and appreciate what actions and parts of the body help them to establish a slow speed, *e.g.* rolls and use of body surfaces, travelling keeping hands and feet only in contact with the floor or apparatus.

It should be remembered that moving at the same speed is tiring. Movement can easily lose its vitality and therefore a change of effort is helpful. The children might, therefore, be asked to select one action and move quickly, then repeat it moving slowly, or choose two different actions and perform one quickly and the other slowly.

2. ACCELERATION AND DECELERATION

The realisation that with certain actions children can move quickly or slowly, makes a natural link to the next stage of developing their Time sense: the development of a feel for acceleration or deceleration within the same or a series of different actions. The latter is more difficult for young children to achieve and could well be a development of the earlier work for nine- and ten-year-olds. The smooth transition from QUICK to SLOW and vice-versa is important in developing fluency and continuity of movement.

Examples of Tasks
1. Walking changing to running, the climax of the increase in speed resulting in a jump or sudden stop.
2. Use hands and feet to travel, start slowly and get quicker.
3. Change between quick and slow as you roll in different ways.
4. Make a phrase of movement where the first and last actions are quick.

3. QUALITATIVE ASPECTS

In developing a qualitative feel for movement, it must be remembered that it is the experience of a sensation, whether one approaches this facet of movement through feeling which is then projected into action, or the reverse, which produces a qualitative response.

The extreme ends of the Time scale may be experienced in movement which has a flash, a momentary sensation and when there is a feeling of

24

fighting against time to produce SUDDEN action. Opposed to this is the sensation of indulging in time where movement is slow motion, SUSTAINED and almost suspended. The latter is not a young child's natural preference, but is something which develops with increasing awareness and control.

Sudden: The experience of suddenness may be given through ideas such as shooting up from the floor or through the idea of "Jack in a Box" when coming off apparatus. All kinds of pouncing and springing actions and the idea of putting a sudden stop to a movement will help to give experience of this quality.

Sustained: Sustained movement may be experienced in actions such as rolling or travelling using hands and feet, linked with the feel of slow motion, taking a long time to transfer the weight from one part of the body to another.

As the children's effort awareness grows, they realise that speed and force are linked. Comprehension that movements can be light, quick or sudden, light, slow and sometimes sustained, or strong and sustained or quick and sudden, enhances their enjoyment and highlights their capacity for resilient rhythmical movement. Children enjoy playing with time patterns and qualifying them with varying degrees of strength.

The Space Factor

Misuse of the Space Factor as a theme for gymnastic work has, on occasion, led to "dancing on apparatus." The space factor is, in fact, revealed through the way in which a person moves in space, and there are two elements. The element of *flexibility* can be seen in movement which has a plasticity in a three-dimensional sense, and there is a *"round-aboutness"* in the movement as a result of indulging in the use of space.

Developing a conscious awareness of this in gymnastic movement is inappropriate, since gymnastic movement tends towards the element of directness through focus on practical doing in relation to apparatus. However, an element of flexibility is associated with twisting and turning, which may be used when weaving in and out of the spaces of a climbing frame or when whipping the legs around the trunk in order to leave an inverted balance.

Changing the focus from HOW one moves to an awareness of WHERE one is moving in space is the main emphasis in gymnastics, and this will be considered in the next chapter.

25

The Flow Factor

As the children have been working, their movements may have been characterised by BOUND flow, revealing a readiness to stop a movement and hold a position at any given moment. On the other hand, there may have been an "on-going" FREE flow quality in the children's efforts, evidenced by their ability to link actions fluently but which they would have found difficult to interrupt suddenly (*see* Figure 7).

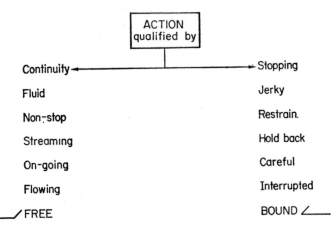

FIG. 7.—The movement vocabulary of the flow factor.

While much of gymnastic work tends towards the element of bound flow because of the necessity for control when moving in relation to apparatus, some focus on the two elements aids not only control but fluency and movement coherence as well.

1. BOUND FLOW

Examples of tasks

1. Ideas such as "move-stop," using different actions, where the teacher might initially control the stops.
2. Moving from one part to another in locomotion with the emphasis on exact, careful placement.
3. Jumping and stressing the arrival in a new place on the floor or on the apparatus.

All these can enhance the feel for bound flow.

26

2. FREE FLOW

Examples of tasks

1. Actions such as leaping, spinning, turning, rolling.
2. Asking the children to move continuously—non-stop.

Both examples can prove exhilarating and promote the feel for movement which is more free-flowing.

Combining the feel for these two elements could be achieved by asking the children to invent a movement sentence, making it clear when they are concerned with interrupting and stopping movement and when they are pursuing the idea of continuity and going.

The provision of appropriate apparatus is important, *e.g.* bars to go around, ropes to swing and turn on, benches to travel along freely or inclined to travel downwards; all can help the children focus on the sense of going. Travelling up against a climbing frame, weaving in and out of the spaces of a window ladder or pulling upwards on an inclined bench enhances the feel of restraint and control.

While the flow of movement begins with the ability to link one action to another in a logical way, the invention of movement sentences becomes more meaningful to children when they become aware of the dynamics of movement. Knowing through feeling how their efforts can fluctuate and vary adds another dimension to the children's experience.

REFERENCES

1. M. Streicher, *Reshaping Physical Education*, Edited by B. Strutt, Manchester University Press, 1970.
2. For detailed study of this topic, readers are referred to *Effort*, by R. Laban and F. C. Lawrence, second edition, 1973, and *Mastery of Movement*, by R. Laban, revised by Lisa Ullmann, 1960, both published by Macdonald and Evans, Ltd.
3. D. G. Pallet, *Modern Educational Gymnastics*, Pergamon Press, 1965, Chapter VIII, p. 52.

CHAPTER IV

SPACE—The Medium of Movement

"ONE of the outstanding contributions of modern physical education is the increased awareness it fosters of spatial dimensions in relation both to one's own body and its environment."[1]

Gymnastics, as part of an on-going programme, is one area where concentration on space can aid movement development and give further scope for inventiveness. As with every other activity, the development of space awareness must build upon a child's pre-school experience.

In his movements, the five-year-old reveals that he has a considerable degree of consciousness where the world of objects is concerned. His movements are increasingly selective and appropriate as a result, in part, of an elemental understanding of certain relationships in space. However, while this pre-school learning is based upon a very real experience—of reaching out and grasping objects, of struggling to attain the vertical, of taking the first steps forward into space and of climbing up and then dropping down— this experience is not enough in itself. If children are to discover space as the medium of movement and appreciate the relationship of spatial reference points, there must be guidance and concentration on spatial aspects.

Developing Space Consciousness

I. THE FEEL FOR SPACE

Initially, the provision of apparatus will provide changing spatial relationships, and therefore in itself will be sufficient challenge to the children.

Space Words: As a first step in developing a child's conscious feel for space, words with a spatial feel such as over, under, around, close to, away from, through, near and far, can be used to stimulate further understanding.

Guided Experience

1. Find three ways of travelling CLOSE TO THE BENCH.
2. Choose a different way of GOING AROUND THE BAR.
3. Show me two ways of travelling ABOVE THE LADDER.

At this point, it may be of value to note that Piaget states that a young child's initial understanding of space is limited to such relationships as close together, apart, above, over, etc., that is, *topological* relationships,[2] and this would appear to support the basic soundness of Laban's concept of space.[3]

2. EXTENSION

Near and Far: In moving, children will naturally use varying degrees of bodily extension in space, from movements which are far from the centre of the body to those which are near to it. As the children change from being stretched, extended, spread out in motion and stillness, to being contracted and curled, the shape of the body will also change from the elementary body shape of large to small.

Developing an awareness of extension into space through the contrast of extremes will help the children appreciate how they can vary the size of their movement, not only in relation to apparatus but also in relation to other children, when they may have to change the size of their movement to avoid or go around them.

Guided Experience
1. "Start with hands and feet close together on the floor—find three different ways of moving where your hands and feet go apart as you extend into space."
2. "Show that you understand the difference between being spread out and being contracted in two different actions."
3. "Travel along the bench—use pouncing and jumping actions which begin small and get bigger."

3. LEVELS

Through working in relation to the floor or apparatus, the children will have been using the three levels of space: High, Medium and Deep. Focussing attention on the different levels is a further step in the development of children's feel for space (*see* Plates 13 and 14).

High: Conscious awareness of movement in the HIGH level can be developed through jumping with awareness of parts of the body going high, *e.g.* head, chest, knees, and that arms can help to swing and lift into the high level. The appropriate take-off is also important and children can discover that the two feet take-off is most helpful here as they thrust

29

themselves away from the floor. In locomotion, children can also discover which parts of their bodies can move into the high level. Different balances can provide further experience of the high level through ideas such as lifting away from, rising high or stretching up and away from a point of balance.

Medium: The MEDIUM level is generally passed *through*, acting as a linking area between the two extremes of high and deep. However, nine- and ten-year-olds enjoy exploring ideas of tilting and leaning into the space around their centres or of bringing their legs parallel to the floor—a "table tops idea." When balancing, for example, on shoulders or head they can pause with their legs in the medium level and then try whipping or spinning actions. Again, when jumping, the idea of bringing their legs up to the medium level can prove a further challenge to their movement mastery.

Deep: Experience of movement in the DEEP level can come through tasks such as "Find ways of moving where all parts of you are close to the floor." Sometimes children may feel they have answered the task but observation may reveal that they have left their hips poking up in the high level! Children may discover that their body is often compact in shape as they move in this level, but need not necessarily remain so.

The provision of apparatus will necessitate a change of level, but children quickly appreciate the difference, for example, between a jump where they simply drop off a box or use a jump to go higher than the box before landing on a mat.

Through moving with the legs in the high level and arms in the deep level, children experience *inversion*, the very essence of gymnastic movement.

4. SPATIAL AREAS

A realisation that the normal reach of the limbs determines a space boundary (known as the kinesphere) which is unique to themselves may spark off further awareness of areas of space in relation to a child's own body centre. Children may appreciate that though their bodily structure naturally divides the space for them, *e.g.* the left leg moving in the space at the left side of the body, they can also move the left leg into the right leg zone, thus adding to the store of movement possibilities. Focus on areas such as in front, behind, to the sides, in addition to above and below can make a further contribution to what Piaget terms the "de-centring process."

Directional Awareness

As the children's movement vocabulary and experience grows, the feel for a more differentiated division of space may be developed. While children have naturally moved in different directions in their previous work, the kinesthetic feel for particular points of orientation towards which they can direct their movements is a further challenge to their mastery of movement in space.

Forwards, Backwards, Up, Down, Right, Left: A first stage towards directional awareness with seven- to eight-year-olds can be in the relationship of their movements to particular points of the room or apparatus, *e.g.* find different ways of TRAVELLING FORWARDS OVER THE BOX, then TRAVEL SIDEWAYS ALONG THE MAT; make a movement UPWARDS TOWARDS THE CEILING, then find a way of travelling BACKWARDS OVER THE MAT. The concept that the surfaces of the body can lead them into the six main directional possibilities is an important stage in the development of the body-space relationship—when rolling backwards, the back surfaces lead, and so on.

This aspect of space can be returned to at a later stage and be developed further. Somewhere between the ages of seven and nine nearly all children come to a spatial understanding of vertical and horizontal co-ordinates. Consequently, by nine years they are capable of relating movement from their body centre towards and away from a reference point in the kinesphere.

Examples of tasks

1. "As you swing from the bar, can you move your legs in two different directions from your centre and then pause?"
2. "Jump from the box and make it clear where your legs are pointing in space."
3. "Travel freely then balance with your free limbs directed towards side right."

Observation can help children to distinguish and name the main directional possibilities. They might then become aware that movement towards points in the backwards area are often neglected.

Pathways

Children in their play often consciously carve out tracks—in the snow, in the sand, along a wall. Discovering that the pathway which the body traces is a movement element which can be consciously manipulated can add to the children's vocabulary of movement in space.

While air patterns play a vital role in the dancer's world, they are less relevant in gymnastics owing to their gestural implications; floor patterns can, however, prove a further challenge to the children's skill and inventiveness.

Children can discover that basically floor patterns may be:

1. Along a line, straight and undeviating.
2. Angular, when two straight lines are joined with a sharp angle, as in a zig-zag.
3. Curving, with a gradual and smooth change in direction as they travel around the curve to form for example, a circle or a letter S.

Examples of tasks

1. "Use different actions as you travel along a line, a bench or a beam—return back along the same path."
2. "Make your own pattern as you move freely over the apparatus (bench, rope and mat)—show clearly when you are using sharp angles and going straight and when you are tracing a curved pathway."
3. "Can you make a zig-zag pattern as you travel on/off/over the bench?"

The space material contained within this chapter, with its initial stress on proximity which then develops into a projectional feel for movement into space, has been recognised as developmentally sound.

While the teaching approach may vary, work with a spatial emphasis should enable children to move with greater clarity and precision when they organise and shape their movement in three-dimensional space as it occurs in the fourth dimension of time.

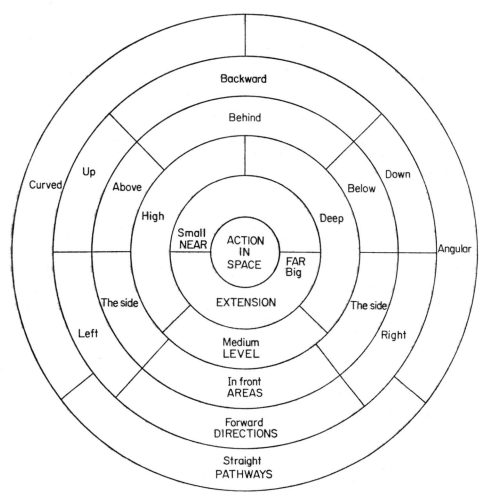

Fig. 8.—Summary of space material.

REFERENCES

1. M. Brearley and E. Hitchfield, *A Teacher's Guide to Reading Piaget*, Routledge and Kegan Paul, 1966, p. 104.
2. B. Inhelder, J. Piaget and A. Szeminska, *The Child's Conception of Geometry*, 1960, and J. Piaget and B. Inhelder, *The Child's Conception of Space*, 1963, both published by Routledge and Kegan Paul.
3. R. Laban, *Modern Educational Dance*, revised by Lisa Ullmann, Macdonald and Evans, Ltd., second edition 1966.

CHAPTER V

Working with Others—a Question of Relationships

Introduction

I. PARTS OF THE BODY

WITH young children, very much concerned with self and coming to terms with their environment, the fact of having to move in relation to apparatus which provides changing spatial situations is a sufficient challenge in itself. An awareness of the RELATIONSHIP of parts of the body to each other can provide a further stimulus to the development of movement potential and may serve as an introduction to partner work. The idea that parts of the body can MEET each other, PART from and PASS or OVERTAKE each other in the air and on the floor in different forms of locomotion can stimulate further exploration and invention.

2. PARTNER WORK

Working with another person (*see* Plate 2) poses an additional problem in relationships, and this area of work should be left until children are more ready to co-operate and share ideas over a period of time. When seven- to eight-year-olds can see several ways of answering a task and are appreciative of another point of view, they are ready to begin on simple ideas.

The keynote of partner work should be that of fun, the enjoyment arising through working together and discovering that new things are possible in movement that would be impossible to achieve alone.

Basically, children may work with or without contact. The idea of working with contact needs careful teaching since in the past it has led to some dubious work involving lifting, lowering, and carrying—this form of partner work can only be justified if, through contact, the partner is able to extend her range of movement. While momentary contact may naturally arise, this aspect of work should generally be left to the secondary stage (eleven years upwards in the United Kingdom).

3. FOUR STARTING SITUATIONS

In partner work, children can begin working in one of the following four situations:

1. One behind the other.
2. Facing each other.
3. Side by side.
4. Back to back.

A situation may be maintained throughout a movement phrase **or** may

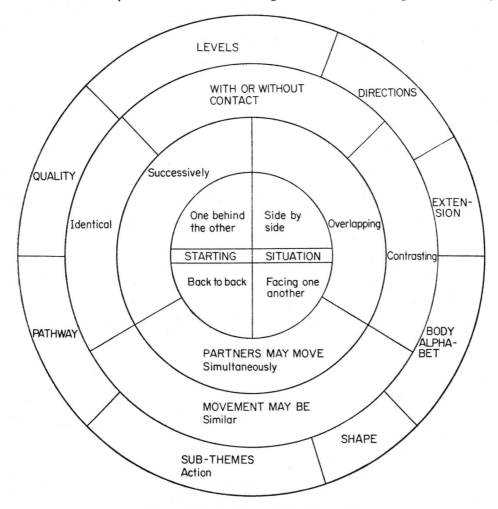

FIG. 9.—The development of partner work.

change as a result of turning or through pathways crossing. In working together, children may move simultaneously, one after the other, *i.e.* successively, or their movements may overlap. Their movements may be identical, similar or contrasting. To follow a partner's movements exactly demands acute observation of such factors as timing, shape, level and pathway and this can prove too much in the early stages of partner work. It is better, therefore, to start exploring the possibilities of partner work using a subsidiary theme which is drawing on the children's past experience. Such themes as body shape, use of levels, aspects of time and directions, can prove a source of inspiration in the new situation.

Ideas for Partner Work

The following ideas may prove helpful in the development of partner work.

1. ONE BEHIND THE OTHER

A follow-the-leader relationship, where the children could follow the same PATHWAY, being left free in the choice of action. A second idea could be to use similar parts of the body, for example, travelling on surfaces one might do a rolling action, whereas the other might do a sliding action.

2. FACING EACH OTHER

This is another simple starting situation, since the children begin with initial visual contact. As a first step, the children begin apart and then explore the possibilities of travelling towards each other in different ways before returning to their own starting point. Secondly, they could move towards each other and then find ways of passing under, over or around. This idea leads to children using each other as "obstacles" either with or without contact.

Older children could also discover the possibilities of moving with a "mirror-like" relationship, *e.g.* A moving to the left while B moves to the right, doing the same movement at the same time.

3. SIDE BY SIDE

Starting in this position, the children could match each other's movements and re-discover which directions are open for them to direct their movement into and which parts of the body lead them into action (*see* Chapter IV).

4. BACK TO BACK

This is a more challenging situation, since the children no longer have vision to assist them in the timing of their actions. It is a relationship which generally demands greater pre-arrangement of movement ideas and is usually linked through the use of turning with one of the three preceding situations. However, children may discover that the sound patterns which emerge as a result of rhythmical phrasing are of significance, in addition to a heightened kinesthetic awareness.

5. PARTNERS ACTING AS AN OBSTACLE OR SUPPORT

This is something which occurs naturally in children's play and can be further developed in gymnastic work. The possibilities are summarised below.

		A	B
		WITHOUT CONTACT	WITH CONTACT
Partner as Obstacle	I	Static	Static
or Support	II	Moving	Moving

Sensitivity and the awareness of appropriate tension and counter-tension is important in the development of working with contact, since this involves moments of active support and counter-balance.

Value of Partner Work

1. OBSERVATION

Through working with a partner, the child's powers of movement observation is challenged and the ability to observe accurately can be gradually developed.

2. MEMORY, CONSISTENCY, ACCURACY AND SELF-DISCOVERY

The repetition of a partner's phrase of movement can not only challenge the movement memory of the observer but demands consistency of repetition from the performer. Partner work can also lead to self-discovery and discovery of habitual movement preferences, for example, of always leading with the right side of the body, or for moving with a particular rhythm.

3. CONFIDENCE

It may also emerge that, while good at taking the lead, a child is less skilful when it comes to following, or that while preferring to follow, a child may develop growing confidence in his own ability through being encouraged to take the initiative.

4. ADAPTABILITY

The showing and sharing of ideas, which can demand the ability to adapt and adjust not only in terms of ideas but also in movement, is yet another facet of movement material which can lead to the extension and enrichment of children's experience.

While partner work may be used as the main theme of a lesson, it should be remembered that children *need time* to pursue movement ideas at their *own rate* and *level*, and therefore opportunity for this should be given at some stage.

Perhaps what is of particular value is that in partner work there is the opportunity to return to familiar material and use it in a new way, *e.g.* linking partner work with different activities—rolling, sliding, turning, jumping; linking partner work with shape, or linking partner work with speed changes. By allowing the opportunity for re-combining, re-shuffling and re-structuring familiar movement material within a new context, an approach is made towards what Koestler terms "bisociative thinking" in his work *The Act of Creation* (Hutchinson and Co., Ltd., 1964).

Plate 9—above left
Leaping.

Plate 10—above right
Developing a rocking action.

Plate 11—below
Asymmetrical preparation for action.

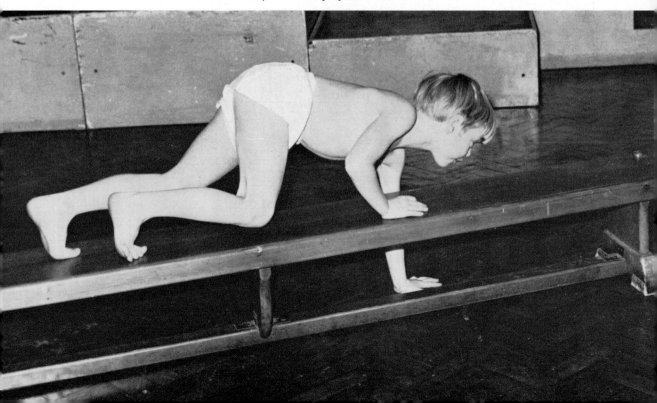

PLATE 12

Flying on to a rope.

PLATE 13
Jumping high.

PLATE 14—LEFT

Hanging while bringing legs up to medium level.

PLATE 15—BELOW

Using a somersault to find balance in medium level.

CHAPTER VI

OBSERVATION—*Teaching from what one sees*

THE crux of successful teaching in Movement Education hinges on the teacher's powers of observation, knowing what to look for; this in turn demands understanding of the material of movement and of children. The effective teacher constantly uses his powers of observation to assess the individuality, mood and needs of the children and then *responds to what he sees*.

While observing children in the light of a movement vocabulary, it should not be forgotten that good observation depends primarily upon use of the senses, involving not only the more obvious senses of sight and sound, but also the muscular or kinesthetic sense. Kinesthetic sympathy enables the observer not only to feel but also to appreciate the quality and complexity of the children's response to a movement task, thus becoming more sensitive to what may be required in the way of further guidance.

Observation By the Teacher

Throughout the lesson, the teacher will be continually assessing the children's movement response, noting their degree of involvement and absorption. Concentration, interest, spontaneity and a variety of response point to the fact that the movement material is satisfying and meeting the needs of the class. On the other hand, there may be a deadness in the children's response, with a loss of interest and concentration in their own activity, which may indicate that the material is inappropriate for the class, that the initial guidance was not sufficiently clear or that the activity had gone on too long. It could even point to a simple ventilation problem!

OBSERVATION therefore becomes THE DETERMINING FACTOR IN MAKING DECISIONS as to when to issue a further challenge, to change the activity or give further guidance and encouragement to the individual child, a small group or the whole class.

Ways of Organising Observation by the Children

Opportunity should be given for the children at some stage of the lesson to observe each other (*see* Plates 16 and 17). Observation should be of work relevant to the chosen theme and could involve one of the following arrangements:

1. HALF THE CLASS MOVING WATCHED BY THE OTHER HALF

This is often useful if one wishes the children to become aware of the richness of response to an initial challenge.

2. A SMALL GROUP MOVING

In floorwork one may use a small group to show contrast in ways of moving—whether of effort, shape, use of the body, etc. A group may be asked to show their work on apparatus because it reveals a variety of response within the group (*see* Plate 8) or a particular quality, or because it may differ from other groups through the nature of the apparatus used.

3. A SINGLE CHILD MOVING

This may be used to focus attention on an original response which reveals clarity and quality of movement and crystallises a particular point during the lesson.

4. OBSERVING A PARTNER

This arrangement is generally left until the children are ready to cope with the demands of partner work (*see* Chapter V). It may become necessary to ask the children to "work with and observe a different partner today," to ensure a general sharing of observation experience.

Observers

During the period of observation, the teacher needs to provide sensitive guidance, to encourage an openness of response which will help to ensure that it is a learning situation. Careful questioning, using words which convey meaning concisely and clearly, will help to refresh the children's memories and serve to reinforce the theme of the lesson.

Regular moments of observation can encourage children in their role as observers. Through a growing knowledge and ability to comment upon and assess the movement response of their fellows, they can make a valuable contribution to the success of any lesson. The children may also come to realise that, while not gifted in movement ability, they may have a special talent for observation—a further step on the way to self-knowledge.

"See and be seen" might well be a good rule for both observers and performers. While watching floorwork presents no problems, apparatus work, where children may need to gather round a particular arrangement, might cause difficulties. A good safety rule might be that the floor is used to sit on, to eliminate the risk of mats or apparatus being accidentally pushed. This also strengthens the concept that APPARATUS IS USED FOR PURPOSEFUL ACTIVITY, and not for resting on.

Performers

When children are asked to show their movement ideas in floorwork, they should be encouraged to sense where to place themselves in space so that their movement is seen in perspective and is not "lost" through moving too close to the class. Perhaps it should be emphasised here that in no way is this a performance *per se*, but *an opportunity to share ideas*. Many young children have a natural penchant for the limelight but others may be more diffident, even self-conscious, and the idea of "sharing" can do much to overcome a possible reluctance to move in front of others.

Repetition of Work

Some guidance may also be helpful as to the number of times that children should repeat their work.

Examples

1. With half the class working, they might be asked to continue working until they hear the words "and rest."
2. A single child might first be asked to perform her phrase once through, and the observers might be asked for comment before the phrase is repeated.
3. A small group could be asked to perform their work three or four times through and then stop.

Criteria for Observation

A word of praise and constructive comment after the children have shown their work can do much to foster the appreciative atmosphere that is conducive to learning. The timing of any period of observation should be well planned, and the criterion for such observation should always be

41

"do the children gain from the movement contribution of others and use it to try out a new movement or modify and clarify their own work?"

Value of Observation

Through observation, the children may become more perceptive, appreciative of skilful movement in others, aware of their own movement preferences and of what they may lack and therefore need to practise.

Training the children's powers of observation—and here the ability to pose the right question is vital—is an important means of learning, through developing a visual sense for movement.

Part Two
Planning, Preparing and Giving a Lesson

CHAPTER VII

Guidelines in Lesson Planning—I: Background Planning

As with every other area of work in the school curriculum, there are certain factors which need to be taken into consideration, whether preparing a single lesson or series of lessons. Not only must the fundamentals of movement be recognised but also the previous experience and present capabilities of the children. Realisation and understanding of the ways in which children learn is a major factor, since this provides the key to the teaching approach.

Stages of Learning

Jumping down, climbing up, balancing, scrambling through spaces, turning upside down, swinging round bars, hanging from branches: these are movement activities which young children enjoy since they are vitally concerned with trying out their own capabilities, testing their own sense for movement and thus coming to terms with their environment.

I. EXPERIMENTATION AND EXPLORATION

EXPERIMENTING with different movements and EXPLORING the environment are basic needs and this is the main core of work with five- to six-year-olds. Apparatus should be provided which allows the children to develop these natural activities. Arising from what the children do, and after their initial burst of exploration, the teacher can give suggestions and pose simple tasks which help them to think about their movement and spark off further experimentation, e.g. "John used hands and feet only as he travelled along the bench, can you use other parts?"

With older children, this period of experimentation, which nevertheless should be dynamic and purposeful, is still a vital part of the lesson. Time, which may be longer or shorter according to the movement idea being explored, must be allowed to enable them to identify the particular aspect of movement they are endeavouring to come to terms with. It should be remembered that this stage will occur not only in floorwork but also in relation to apparatus.

45

2. REPETITION

The need to repeat movement for its own sake is seen at a very early stage. Through repetition, children gain the necessary "feel" for an action and enjoy the flow of movement. While exactness of repetition is not looked for in the early stages, repetition helps young children to sense the rhythm inherent in movement and to develop their movement memory.

3. SELECTION

A vital stage arrives when the child himself selects, or is asked to choose, from his growing movement vocabulary actions which are appropriate to the task in hand. Questions such as "How do you begin?" or "Choose an action and move QUICKLY" all help the child to become more selective in his movement response.

When children have reached the stage of linking actions to form a movement sequence and have the ability to repeat it, there is greater opportunity for movement development.

4. CLARIFICATION AND MASTERY

Guidance, which may be in the form of questioning, observation or a further challenge, is necessary to help the children in the process of developing and refining their efforts in relation to the theme of the lesson.

This harnessing of children's inventive powers, where ideas are realised in terms of action and where the process of formulation is allied with performance, is a vital component of purposeful work. It is helpful to give the children a reminder as to the nature of their task before they finally master it and "do what they mean to do."

Neglect of any of these ways of learning can lead to frustration, poverty of response and a fragmentary experience which can deny the child the opportunity of discovering his own sense for movement.

Floor and Apparatus Work

It is a basic need of young children to be able to move in relation to obstacles, and the provision of apparatus can do much to satisfy this need.

A variety of apparatus allows children to satisfy their need to climb, hang, swing, jump and balance, and is a means whereby their natural mobility can be maintained and their movement range extended. Through the use of apparatus, new and challenging spatial situations are created which provide a fresh and stimulating learning environment. Characteristic of the "new" approach has been the combining of different pieces of apparatus to form a unit for group activity, *e.g.* linking a box, bench, rope and mat.

With young children, who already spend a considerable part of the day in moving from one activity to another in a relatively free way, the major part of the lesson will be spent in exploring and discovering new movement possibilities on the apparatus.

From seven years upwards, when children begin to spend longer periods of time in a more confined situation, floorwork becomes an increasingly valuable part of the lesson, serving initially as a transition stage in awakening the body-mind. Introducing a new movement idea or developing the theme of a previous lesson without apparatus allows the children to work out movement ideas unhampered by the additional problems that can be posed by apparatus. As they develop a longer span of concentration, the children are more able to sustain interest in floorwork and are capable of inventing phrases of movement which give them considerable enjoyment and satisfaction.

It should not be forgotten that the whole point of gymnastic work is that TIME IS SPENT IN MOVING ON APPARATUS. There should be a realisation that the ideas experimented with and worked out on the floor must be translated and developed in relation to apparatus. Here it should be recognised that the physical environment provided by the apparatus and its placement will in part determine the movement response. For example, a climbing frame will determine actions such as climbing and swinging. From the "input" phase in the development of skilful movement, the problem for the children becomes one of deciding in what ways they can utilise the experience gained in floorwork on the apparatus.

I. THE USE OF SMALL APPARATUS

Small apparatus should only be used for gymnastic work if it helps to create a space which can be moved through or if it provides an obstacle which can be moved on, off or over. Hoops, car tyres, canes, skittles, ropes, stage blocks, tables and chairs can all be used in various ways to supplement gymnastic apparatus where it is in short supply.

Teachers of this age group can do much to badger those in authority to supply gymnastic apparatus, since it is between the ages of five to eleven years, rather than at the adolescent stage, that the majority of children most enjoy this form of movement activity.

2. HANDLING APPARATUS

Children enjoy fixing things, and from the very first lesson they should be given the responsibility of helping to erect, arrange and clear away apparatus quietly and efficiently (*see* Plates 21 and 22). Awareness of the principles involved in gripping, lifting, carrying and lowering forms an integral part of their movement education, not only to guard against the possibility of bodily strain but to prevent damage to what can be expensive apparatus.

2. SAFETY RULES

1. When *lifting* benches, *two children* should *work together using both hands to lift* the bench *simultaneously*. As on all occasions concerned with lifting a heavy object, understanding of why they need to bend their knees and use their powerful leg muscles to avoid strain on the lower back should be an integral part of their movement education.

2. *Mats* should be stacked according to size and type and handles should be used for carrying them if provided. Getting corners and edges to match is something which children enjoy, but time must be allowed for this. Again, two people working together avoid mats being dragged along the floor.

3. Teach children to *push and not pull* apparatus on wheels, with one person placed at the side to act as an additional guide. This should safeguard the apparatus being pulled on to toes should the lifting device fail.

4. Show children the *correct sequence of movements* when erecting the more complicated apparatus, *e.g.* cave-type apparatus, and give them the opportunity to practice. This will help towards saving valuable working time in subsequent lessons.

It is usually helpful if the same children who erected the major apparatus also clear it away.

A frequent comment from overseas visitors or people experiencing this work for the first time has been "What about safety? Where are the spotters, the catchers?"

48

The answer to these queries lies in the fact that the children would not be moving with such a degree of inventiveness and control if they did not have complete confidence in their own ability. Safety is built-in, and this facility is developed through the children's own learning experiences which enable them to identify those factors which contribute to skilful body management. Knapp's comment[1] on the question of manual guidance is also of some relevance:

> "In general it is not desirable, because the kinaesthetic sensations felt by the learner will be different from those he experiences when performing on his own and there is also the risk that he will adopt a passive attitude which is never conducive to learning."

This does not, however, preclude any child from asking either the teacher or another child to help him should the need arise. Observation and an understanding of elementary mechanics should enable a teacher to identify where a child may need support. For example, a child hanging upside down from a rope may be given hand support under the shoulder and on the hips. Since a detailed exposition of support techniques is considered to be outside the scope of this book for the reasons already stated, readers are referred to the book by T. S. Cochrane listed at the end of the chapter.[2]

4. ORGANISATION AND PROVISION

Perhaps the first consideration to be made is whether to have groups of children working on different arrangements of apparatus or whether to have children working simultaneously on the same type of apparatus, *e.g.* benches, mats, ropes. The latter arrangement, sometimes known as Class Activities, will depend largely on whether there is sufficient apparatus available to allow for maximum participation by the class.

Whichever method is used, the choice and arrangement of apparatus must be related to the movement needs and abilities of the class and the theme of the lesson.

5. FURTHER GUIDELINES

1. Provide apparatus which is not only *appropriate* to the children's abilities but which also *enhances the theme* of the lesson. For example, when exploring asymmetry, placing mats to one side of a box or a bench and mats at different angles to a single rope can help

children in the task of making one side of the body more active than the other.

2. *Pathways* towards and away from apparatus should be planned so that approach and landing areas do not coincide with adjacent groups, thus helping to avoid the possibility of collisions. A diagram showing how the apparatus is to be set out and which indicates pathways is an integral part of lesson preparation.

3. When moving round from one unit of apparatus to another, the next unit should involve a *change of bodily activity*. For example, an arrangement where the main emphasis has been on running and jumping should be followed by a unit demanding a different bodily use, *e.g.* climbing or swinging.

4. Consider the use of the *floor* as a *linking area* in relation to a single piece of apparatus and to a unit of apparatus, since this is often neglected when children are developing movement sentences. The "all-round" approach also helps to avoid queues.

At this point it might be appropriate to mention the practice of erecting apparatus at the beginning of a morning or afternoon session regardless of the stages of development and movement themes being worked on by different groups of children. This practice is to be deplored since it runs counter to the whole concept of current educational thought and also disregards the fact that children enjoy fixing things. In addition, with the lightweight apparatus that is specially designed for this work there should not be a handling problem. The fact that the apparatus is always the same may also lead to a general "fed-upness" on the part of the children, since no fresh challenge is provided by the arrangement of apparatus.

6. PROGRESSION IN THE USE OF APPARATUS

It should be appreciated that a form of progression can be made through the following:

1. *Adding* a piece of apparatus. If children have been working on a class activity using mats only, a bench could be added; if using benches, a hoop or box could be added, and so on. This way of working can prove helpful when introducing a new movement idea, using a piece of apparatus for the first time or when working

with young children who may be unused to gymnastic work and handling apparatus.

2. Making the apparatus *higher* or *enlarging the space* between different pieces of apparatus.

3. Allocating children floor space and apparatus but allowing them to *arrange it themselves*.

4. *Changing from one unit of apparatus to another*, which allows for the further development of their movement ability. For example, exploring the feel of SUDDEN action through the ideas of arriving on and SHOOTING OFF a box, contrasted with finding different ways of travelling SLOWLY along a bench. With older children, a unit of box, bench and mat could be used to develop jumping, pouncing and balancing, contrasted with a unit of two ropes and a bench where they add spinning to their previous ideas.

Group Work

The whole point of the lesson is that TIME IS SPENT IN ACTIVITY, therefore numbers should be kept small to enable each child to gain as much movement experience as possible *on apparatus*. Four to six children per group allows for this, while generally proving sufficient to handle a unit of apparatus.

REFERENCES

1. B. Knapp, *Skill In Sport*, Routledge and Kegan Paul, 1963, p. 25.
2. T. S. Cochrane, *International Gymnastics for Girls and Women*, Addison-Wesley, 1969.

CHAPTER VIII

Guidelines in Lesson Planning—II: Selection of Content

PERHAPS the first problem facing a teacher when planning a lesson or series of lessons is the question of "what to teach?" The choice of content is not always a simple matter, since such factors as the children's previous experience, their movement ability and their movement needs must be taken into account. The essential consideration is to select material which will develop the children's movement potential and widen their experience.

Summary of Material: Four Major Areas of Movement

1. The development of BODY AWARENESS, where words will be used which relate to activity, the body alphabet, right and left sides and shape.
2. Concentration on HOW the body moves, using words which focus on the Weight and Time factors and the rhythmical aspect of movement.
3. Attention to SPACE, and use of words which focus on extension, size, levels, directions and pathways.
4. The RELATIONSHIP element, where not only awareness of parts to the whole is developed, but the ability to share movement ideas is fostered.

Theme and Sub-theme in Relation to Action

In lesson planning, one generally pinpoints a specific aspect of movement from one of the four major areas to act as the main movement idea or theme of the lesson. A different yet related facet of movement may be used to underline this. Whatever the chosen theme, a teacher must remember that movement, and therefore gymnastics, IS A LANGUAGE OF ACTION, and accordingly must consider how the selected idea can develop in terms of action. It may be decided that experience of TIME in a variety of BODILY ACTIONS would be appropriate for the class. The theme might be further developed through awareness of the body alphabet.

52

The lesson material could then be set out in the following way with the main ideas being simply outlined in point form:

FLOORWORK

1. FREE PRACTICE of different actions, *e.g.* jumping, rocking, sliding.
2. TIME—QUICK/SLOW. Choose an action, can you travel at different speeds? Quickly? Slowly?
3. Travel on HANDS and FEET only, what different actions can you perform travelling Quickly? Slowly?
4. Use other parts of the body to receive your weight, can you travel at DIFFERENT SPEEDS?
5. FORMULATE A SENTENCE OF ACTION. Use two *quick* actions and one *slow* action.

APPARATUS WORK

Examples of tasks

1. *Bench, mat.* Discover different ways of travelling along QUICKLY, SLOWLY.
2. *Two mats, box top.* Experiment with balancing on different body parts. Can you change from one balance to another QUICKLY? SLOWLY?

From this example, it can be seen that all movement exploration and teacher guidance directs the child's attention to the main movement idea of the lesson. The use of a sub-theme drawn from already familiar material enables a teacher to "coach into" or draw from the main theme. In addition, it can also help to safeguard the inexperienced from being at a complete loss over material.

In the early stages, many teachers often fail to appreciate the richness of a movement idea, and either exhaust their material in one lesson or else throw in everything they can remember about movement analysis. When the latter happens, any skill the children may have attained is often dissipated through confusion of ideas and lack of focus. At other times, they fail to recognise the richness of the children's movement response. A more detailed preparation (*see* Chapter IX) can do much towards overcoming this problem, although it is readily admitted that lesson planning does not guarantee automatic success!

Lesson Evaluation

Teachers may find it difficult to assess a lesson where the children's response is so transient and where they have to rely on observation and movement memory. Nevertheless, an evaluation should be made if teaching is to be effective and if the children are to make progress in terms of movement ideas and mastery. Certain criteria common to any lesson can provide guidelines, in addition to an awareness of particular points relevant to gymnastic work.

1. CHANGING

Were the children able to change quickly with the minimum time lost? Was sufficient time allowed for changing and showering at the end of the lesson?

2. ORGANISATION

Was the apparatus in the best place for ease of access and distribution? Were the children able to handle the apparatus quietly, safely and efficiently?

3. CONTENT

Was the work presented in such a way that all the children were able to achieve satisfaction and enjoyment? Note here positive progress made by the whole class, and by particular children.

If the children were not working with interest, confidence and understanding, was this due to:

1. The movement content being too difficult or too easy for the class and/or individuals at their particular stage of development?
2. Lack of the appropriate verbal clues or questions in relation to the chosen theme?
3. Failure to allow sufficient time for exploration, repetition, etc.?

PLATE 16—ABOVE
Five-year-olds observing a cartwheel.

PLATE 17—BELOW
Observing a crab-like action.

PLATE 18—LEFT
A five-year-old's way of climbing on to a beam.

PLATE 19—BELOW
Speed changes while moving on large surfaces.

PLATE 20—RIGHT
The enjoyment of hanging from the beam prior to leading with the left side on to the mat.

PLATE 21—BELOW
Assembling a unit of apparatus.

4. Lack of contrast in terms of activity and action?

5. Lack of insistence on the movement task being fulfilled?

4. MOVEMENT OBSERVATION

Were opportunities used for developing the children's powers of observation, where appropriate? Was the questioning purposeful, followed by immediate opportunities for practice?

5. APPARATUS

How many groups did the children use? Will there be any progression needed in the use of apparatus, *e.g.* add a piece, make it higher? Was the apparatus appropriate for the particular movement task?

6. CONCLUSION

The above points can go some way towards building up a movement picture of the children's responses, and should reveal whether there was evidence of new thinking in movement and movement mastery, and should point the way to the development of work in succeeding lessons.

The Teaching Approach

It has been said that "the skilful teacher withdraws herself and throws the burden of discovery and explanation upon the children."[1] This does not mean, however, the abandonment of responsibility to the class, since creative work can never be left to chance. The freedom to be creative can only be attained through the discipline of a framework designed to release creativity. The teacher's role is, therefore, to structure situations which will allow children to be inventive and develop their movement resources and to encourage, inspire and guide the children in a variety of ways during the working period.

The setting of movement problems has caused some physical educationists to label Movement Education as "Problem-solving." This misconception has occurred when there has been a failure to distinguish between the teaching approach on the one hand and the movement material on the other. One could equally well teach the material in a direct way and indeed, on occasion, it may be more valuable to do so. However, if teachers believe that a child should be creative and inventive in his movement response, then the methods of achieving this will be mainly through problem-solving and guided discovery.

1. PROBLEM SOLVING

The problem-solving approach allows for many answers to a movement problem. To the question, "what parts of the body can you balance on?" the movement response might be in terms of the head, shoulders, one knee, hands or a foot. The children might go on to discover that some parts of the body are more helpful to balance on than others and that the smaller the point of balance becomes the greater is the challenge to their movement mastery. For the children, there is always the possibility of finding a new way of moving or balancing, or a new variation.

The element of choice which is fundamental to this approach strengthens the children's motivation and through this they gain a greater sense of achievement and satisfaction in doing. The discovery that their own unique movement response is of value and concern to the teacher, generates a greater sense of confidence in their own abilities since they are no longer measured by a set of arbitrary and pre-determined standards.

2. GUIDED DISCOVERY

With guided discovery, there is a need to pose questions and provide clues in a logical order. To discover the five basic jumps one could ask "can you show me what jumping is?" The response will vary, but all will leave the floor at some point.

Observation might follow, "look at Mary and John. In what way do they differ in their take-off and landing?" Answer: "Mary jumped from both feet and landed on both feet, John used only one foot—he hopped!"

A further question "are these the only possibilities?" should bring the answer—in movement—that there are three more basic variations. The discovery of the five basic jumps should be reinforced by opportunity for immediate practice to strengthen the learning situation. Arising from the question "which of these jumps gives a feel for continuity and going, which jump gives more of a feel for stopping?" a further discovery can be made about action and the FLOW factor.

With this approach, the children are still involved in decision-making but the element of choice is considerably restricted. Knowing the desired end, one needs to think in reverse and formulate questions and clues which will lead to a well-defined response.

From discovery of the basic jumps which, in one sense, was a narrowing down process, the children could be given a task: "make up a sequence using these basic jumps." The possible combinations and right answers are endless!

While both these teaching approaches help children to make movement decisions, to discover and invent movement and to develop an awareness that movement responses need to be relevant, it should not be forgotten that there may be a moment where direct teaching is required.

3. DIRECT TEACHING

The direct approach might involve observing a child perform a movement and then asking the children to copy it. It could be a verbal directive of what to do and how to do it.

Although this approach does not give the children the opportunity of active decision-making and there is no element of choice, it should not be forgotten that on occasion it can be of value. Concentration on a specific way of performing a movement can prove a challenge to children and supply a different kind of discipline which can be at the same time enjoyable. It can give confidence to children who may feel insecure when presented with too wide a choice and at the same time prove a starting point for further movement discovery. On occasion, direct teaching can be a factor in establishing safe and controlled movement. It is, however, readily appreciated that the teaching approach is only illuminated when seen in the context of the lesson, and that it is inseparable from a number of other factors.

A good teacher will use a combination of methods, since no single approach is bound to be right for all children, or even all teachers! However, while so much can depend upon the immeasurable and the intangible, sensitive guidance and a readiness to be flexible, together with the ability to structure a movement situation which is essentially open-ended are fundamental if a child is to discover something of his own movement potential. Above all, an atmosphere where a sense of fun prevails through the sharing of ideas can do much towards providing for a meaningful movement experience.

REFERENCES

1. Beatrice and Arnold Gesell, *The Normal Child and Primary Education*, Ginn, 1912, p. 308. *From:* E. Lawrence, *The Origins and Growth of Modern Education*, Penguin, 1970, p. 338.

CHAPTER IX

Lesson Plans

Introduction

THE following lesson outlines are offered as guidelines for providing a more structured learning situation. Their sole purpose is to provide a possible framework, indicating the way in which a movement theme might be developed through floorwork to the climax on apparatus.

The sample plans outline lesson material drawn from each of the four major areas which form the cognitive structure of movement and they are suggested for use with the different age groups.

Examples are given of clues, questions and movement tasks designed to focus the children's attention on the main theme, with possible responses. Classes of thirty to forty children will obviously require more units of apparatus than the number given in the plans but, since the apparatus available will determine what these could be, it was felt that teachers could devise their own additional units. The conclusion of the lesson has been omitted since it was felt that it could be left for the teacher to find her own inspiration! However, it should be recognised that clearing away is an integral part of the lesson, the rounding-off contributing to the unity of the whole and acting as a transition to the succeeding activity.

It is hoped that these lesson outlines will enable some teachers to begin, help others to continue their work with children and spark off yet others to fresh thinking. The ideal is that teachers will eventually formulate their own lesson plans which, while retaining an understanding of basic principles, will reflect their own personality and the needs of the children they teach.

4–6 Years

While young children will enter spontaneously and wholeheartedly into all forms of movement activity, there is often little or no clear-cut separation of one movement form from another. At one moment, a child will use a hoop in a games-like way and the next moment it becomes a magic space to move into. A box is fun to jump off from but it also might become an imaginary horse to ride! The provision of a stimulating environment which offers scope for a variety of movement responses is therefore important.

Exploration of Movement Ideas

It is suggested that simple ideas be explored with the children which, according to their needs of the moment, might stimulate and develop movement which on the one hand may be more expressive and dance-like or on the other hand be more concerned with practical activity. As examples, the following action words and simple phrases could be a starting point for further movement exploration:

Jumping, hopping, bobbing, gripping, contracting, curling, spreading, stretching, spinning, whirling, collapsing, rolling, weaving, crawling.

Run and hover, spin and grip; roll and pause, curl then spread out and balance; skim along, shoot up then stop; crouch along then pounce, leap up and fly.

The working space could be organised in such a way that one area could be used for pursuing movement on apparatus, the central space could perhaps be utilised as an area where children could explore moving with percussion instruments and a further area could be used for experimentation with a variety of objects and implements. Any throwing of balls could be directed towards the end wall.

Young children are able to exercise a considerable degree of self-direction and at this stage they are very much concerned with exploring their own effort capabilities. For this reason, time must be allowed for the children not only to explore but repeat movements as many times as they feel is necessary for them. The use of discerning observation will enable the teacher to give guidance to the children arising from their activities. Questions such as "can you find another way of travelling? jumping? going over?" can stimulate further discovery; "try that again, which part of you arrived first?" can help children to recall and develop an inner awareness of what they have been doing.

As the children become increasingly confident in moving freely and spontaneously in relation to a variety of gymnastic apparatus, it should be recognised that children will not be content merely to practise "moving."

The presence of gymnastic apparatus provides a specific frame of reference for the development of movement ideas which are essentially gymnastic in character.

5–6 Years

Lesson Content: 1

The exploration of basic activities.

FLOORWORK GUIDANCE

The children begin by moving in their own space. They might start from different positions, *e.g.* standing, sitting, kneeling; encourage the children to find different ways of moving. The answer may come in the form of turns, spins, jumping or simply stretching and curling.

1. CLARIFY. Ask the children to choose one way of moving and repeat it three times then hold still.
2. OBSERVE. What is the main difference between John's and Peter's movement? Answer—John left the floor—he jumped.
3. TRAVEL WITH DIFFERENT JUMPS, SKIPS. Make your feet send you off the floor. How do you jump high? Which body parts help you? Are you using both feet? One foot? One foot then two?
4. Work in your own space. FIND DIFFERENT WAYS OF TURNING, SPINNING. Which parts of your body help you to spin? Did you stay at the same speed all the time?
5. Use different parts of your body to HELP YOU TO TRAVEL to a new place, *e.g.* hands, seat, surfaces. Actions such as rolling, sliding, crawling, bunny hops will result, *i.e.* LOCOMOTION.

FORMULATE

Choose two different actions and make a sentence of action.

APPARATUS WORK

Examples of cues to encourage the use of different activities after initial experimentation.

1. *Bench, mat.* Find different actions that you can do as you travel along. Can you turn, spin at some point? Can you slide and roll?

2. *Box, mat, hoop.* Placed on the floor approximately three to four feet from the mat, the gap being designed to encourage jumping and springing actions.

3. *Climber.* Can you find different actions? Can you hang then swing? Can you put in a turn at some point?

4. *Ropes, mats.* Can you move up your rope? Can you run then turn? Which parts of the body help you to swing? Hold still?

Lesson Content: 2

Extension into space. Developing the feel for movements which extend and stretch out into space, contrasted with those which take place near the body centre.

FLOORWORK GUIDANCE

1. WORK IN YOUR OWN SPACE. Find ways in which you can make yourself very small then change and make yourself very big. Make your movement GROW INTO SPACE, stretch out and THEN SHRINK, curl up, become small.

2. STEPPING, RUNNING AND JUMPING FREELY. Can you change the SIZE of your actions? Big steps? Tiny steps? Big jumps? Little jumps? Feet stepping far away from each other then moving close to each other—find different ways.

3. FIND OTHER WAYS OF TRAVELLING. *E.g.,* rolling, travelling on hands and feet only. Can you STRETCH OUT as you travel? Can you do the opposite, CONTRACT, TUCK-UP AND MAKE YOURSELF SMALL as you travel?

APPARATUS WORK

With young children, the provision of apparatus is often sufficiently stimulating in itself and no further challenge may be needed. Some children may show a readiness to pursue this theme on the apparatus. Recognition of this fact and a readiness to give further cues which relate to the underlying

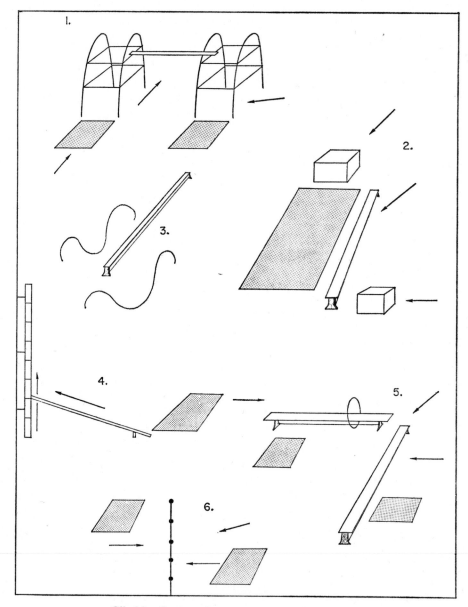

1 Climbing frame unit, two mats.
2 Two stage blocks, bench, mat.
3 Bench (balance side up) two skipping ropes.
4 Bench inclined to the second rung of a climbing frame.
5 Two benches with a large hoop fixed vertically at some point, two mats.
6 Climbing rope, two mats.

Fig. 10.—Possible arrangements of apparatus in the work space. Arrows indicate possible lines of approach to the apparatus.

theme of the lesson serve to reinforce the learning situation and may encourage other children to try out new ideas. For example, "good—now can you stretch out into space as you balance?" or "can you tuck-up in space as you travel along the mat, in and out of the climber?" "can you shoot out into space as you jump off the box?"

The arrangement shown in Figure 10 allows for a variety of movement experience and recognises the fact that some schools may not have much in the way of gymnastic apparatus. The arrows indicate possible lines of approach to each piece of apparatus.

6–7 Years

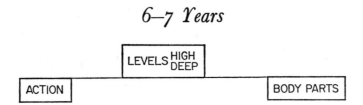

Lesson Content: 1

Exploration of the feel for moving in the contrasting levels of DEEP and HIGH.

FLOORWORK GUIDANCE

1. The children begin by TRAVELLING FREELY with the emphasis on using all the space as they move in, out and around each other: "can you go UP AND DOWN as you travel? let your HEAD LEAD THE WAY—sometimes high, sometimes low." Find different ways. DIP, DIVE, THEN SHOOT UP, JUMP HIGH.

2. Can you move with your WHOLE BODY CLOSE TO THE FLOOR? Find different actions that you can do in this DEEP SPACE, *e.g.* slide, roll, pull, push yourself along.

3. Work in your own space, FIND A PART THAT YOU CAN BALANCE ON. Can you stretch up INTO THE HIGH SPACE? Can you lift yourself away from that part? Make it a HIGH BALANCE, UP TO THE CEILING. Change to another part, lift yourself high then SQUASH YOURSELF DOWN LOW. Try this idea two or three times.

4. JUMPING. Which parts of your body HELP YOU TO GO HIGH? Can knees, feet go into the high space? Find other actions where feet can go high.

63

FORMULATE

Make a sentence of action where you show me that you can go HIGH then travel DEEP.

APPARATUS WORK

Examples of tasks.

1. *Climber, bench, mat.* Can you sometimes go high then deep as you travel along, in and out of the spaces?
2. *Two benches.* Use one bench and work in the deep level, keep close to it. Can you find three different actions? Use the second bench and find different parts that you can take high.
3. *Box, two hoops, two mats.* Find different actions that you can do as you move on, off, over the apparatus. Can you put in a balance—make it clear whether you are stretched up high or curled and squashed deep.

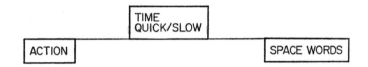

Lesson Content : 2

The development of the feel for quickness and slowness in a variety of bodily actions.

FLOORWORK GUIDANCE

Children in a space. Travel QUICKLY over the floor—and stop. Can you find another way of travelling quickly? and another?

OBSERVATION

With the teacher, half the class observe the other half working, noting the kind of actions which are appropriate to moving quickly, *e.g.* jumping, running, rolling, pouncing actions.

GUIDANCE

1. Children experiment further, but ask that they put a stop every so often, *i.e.* "move quickly and stop," the stop enabling them to recharge their energy.

2. Ask the children to find different ways of travelling SLOWLY, to feel every part moving slowly over the floor. Choose another action, can you make it Slow Motion? Through experimentation, the children may discover the kind of actions where they can move quickly or slowly and that certain actions, for example, rolling actions, may be performed either quickly or slowly.

FORMULATE

Children invent a sentence of movement containing two different actions, move close to the floor and away from the floor. Make it clear when you are moving QUICKLY, SLOWLY.

APPARATUS WORK

Examples of group tasks.

1. *Climber, mats.* Children discover different ways of moving QUICKLY or SLOWLY as they travel through the spaces or move away from and close to the climber.
2. *Two benches in* V *arrangement.* Discover ways of travelling on and off one bench QUICKLY—on the other SLOWLY.
3. *Springboard, mat.* Running and jumping. Can you finish with a SLOW action when you come down on to the mat?
4. *Box top, mat.* Get on in your own way. Can you shoot off QUICKLY? or can you find ways of travelling along the box QUICKLY? SLOWLY?

7 Years

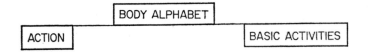

Lesson Content: 1

Exploration of what different parts of the body contribute to **action** and **stillness**.

FLOORWORK

TRAVEL ON FEET ONLY. Can you find DIFFERENT PARTS of your feet to move on? To STOP AND HOLD STILL? *E.g.,* toes, heels, ball of foot?

1. The children may become aware that while they naturally use a heel, ball, toe movement when walking, in *jumping* the ball of the foot and toes are particularly important.

2. WORK IN YOUR OWN SPACE. JUMP UP AND DOWN FOUR TIMES THEN STOP. Which part of your foot is important? Where is your weight when you begin? Which part leads the way as you land? Do that again—show that you can use the BALL OF YOUR FOOT AND YOUR TOES TO MAKE SPRINGY JUMPS AND SOFT LANDINGS.

3. "Good, now can you make a part of you IMPORTANT IN THE AIR? Your head? a knee, elbows?"

4. CHANGE FROM JUMPING TO STEPPING. "Can you step from your feet on to OTHER PARTS OF YOUR BODY?"
   The most natural response will be to step on to hands and combine hands and feet, *e.g.* in crab-walk (*see* Plate 17), cartwheels. Encourage the children to find other parts which they can step on to, *e.g.* knees, elbows, hips.

5. "Can you travel on DIFFERENT PARTS THEN HOLD STILL, BALANCE? Do this several times." Which parts are EASY to balance on? MORE DIFFICULT?

FORMULATE

Use the idea of step-like actions and jumping to make a movement sentence. Make it clear which parts of your body are important in the air, on the floor.

APPARATUS WORK

Examples of group tasks.

1. *Climber, inclined plank, mat.* Can you make STEP-LIKE ACTIONS with hands and feet as you travel on the climber? USE HANDS ONLY? ONE HAND, TWO FEET?

2. *Hoops placed on the floor.* The children could explore the idea of beginning with hands placed inside the hoops while they try walking their feet around the outside, or they might jump in and out then step across in different ways.

3. *Ropes to swing on and climb up.* The children can discover which parts

of the body can be used to grip the rope while other parts may move in space.

4. *Bench, a horse, two mats.* Find your own way of making "step-like" actions along the bench, use contrasting actions on the horse, mats.

5. *Box, mats.* Experiment with moving and stopping. Can you use three different parts to balance on?

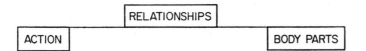

Lesson Content: 2

The development of a feel for the relationship of parts of the body to each other.

FLOORWORK

Find your own space. Can you travel using your feet in different ways? *e.g.,* on toes, heels, stepping and jumping.

EXPLORATION OF RELATIONSHIPS

1. Can you find ways of travelling where your feet COME TOGETHER, MEET, and go APART? Can one foot CATCH UP with the other? CHASE IT?

2. USE HANDS AND FEET ONLY. Can you find ways of travelling where hands and feet go APART, MEET, OVERTAKE, and go AROUND each other?

   Allow time for the children to experiment and give further guidance as necessary.

OBSERVATION

In small groups, children watch each other working and discover any new actions that they may not have thought of while working on this movement idea. Allow them time to perform any new movements.

GUIDANCE

Children working in their own space. Can you balance on different parts? As you balance, can you move different parts of your body TOWARDS each other, AWAY FROM or AROUND each other?

APPARATUS WORK

Examples of group tasks.

1. *Two benches, mat.* Can you find ways of travelling on hands and feet where they come together and move apart?
2. *Climber.* Can you find ways of moving where parts of your body come together, go apart, move around each other?
3. *Springboard, mat.* Can you find different jumps where feet, knees go apart, meet in the air?
4. *Horse, bench, mat.* Explore the idea of feet and hands going around each other at some point.
5. *Box, two mats.* Can you find ways of moving where hands and feet pass each other?

Lesson Content : 3

Exploration of partner work using space words.

FLOORWORK

The children to begin working on actions that take them CLOSE to the floor then change to actions that take them AWAY FROM the floor, *e.g.* rolling, sliding, travelling on hands and feet contrasted with different jumps.

PARTNER WORK: IDEAS FOR BEGINNING WORK

1. Work with a partner. "Begin CLOSE to your partner, FACING EACH OTHER. Take it in turns to do an action that will take you AWAY FROM YOUR PARTNER then change to an action which will bring you BACK AGAIN. A moves, then B moves." Once the children have grasped the idea, encourage them to use different actions and to observe carefully how far away, and how close together, their partner's action takes them before they respond with their own action.

2. Start with a SPACE BETWEEN YOU. "Can you find a way of going OVER, UNDER each other? A first, then B?" Observe carefully and

help the children to appreciate the kind of adjustments they may need to make in their own movement, *e.g.* A is jumping over B, what must B do?—go into a small tucked shape, and so on.

APPARATUS WORK

Examples of guidance

1. *Two box tops, two mats placed between them.* Use different actions as you travel OVER, CLOSE TO, AWAY FROM the apparatus. The children to decide whether they want to work with a partner or not (some children may be ready to continue with the idea of partner work others may need more time to work as an individual).

2. *Two benches, three mats.* Work with a partner and find ways of working AWAY FROM AND TOWARDS EACH OTHER as you travel on, off, over the bench and mats.

3. *Climber.* As you climb up and down and go through the spaces is there a moment when you might do the SAME ACTION AS YOUR PARTNER?

4. *Essex stools, two inclined planks, two mats.* The children might continue with the idea of moving towards a partner, A moving, then B moving up the plank, each being free in their choice of action and in determining whether to PASS EACH OTHER on the apparatus, or to RETURN TO THEIR STARTING POINT.

7–8 Years

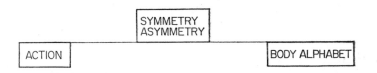

Lesson Content

Developing a feel for symmetry and asymmetry in motion and stillness.

FLOORWORK GUIDANCE

Ask the children to explore the idea of MATCHING BOTH SIDES of the body, DOING THE SAME as they travel then balance.

EXPLORATION OF SYMMETRY

1. Encourage them to experience the feel of symmetry in different activities (*e.g.*, while jumping, travelling on hands and feet or rolling)—of both feet, both knees, both hands doing the same.
2. Ask half the class to watch the other half working. "What kind of TAKE-OFF and LANDING helps these symmetrical actions?" Two feet–two feet?
3. The children continue working—to feel the evenness of the two feet–two feet take-off and landing, of RIGHT and LEFT sides doing the same as they travel and balance.

EXPLORATION OF ASYMMETRY

"What is the opposite of MATCHING, EVEN movement? Show me in your actions." The response should be in terms of TIPPING, TILTING, the right leg reaching further than the left, the left side contracting while the right side extends while travelling balancing and so on. Be ready to suggest ideas for the children to try out.

APPARATUS WORK

Example of group tasks.

1. *Two benches, two mats.* The children explore symmetrical actions as they travel along or on and off the first bench. On the second bench the children to find what actions they can do where tipping, tilting and pushing off to the right or left are stressed.
2. *Box top, two mats.* "Can you make symmetrical even shapes in the air as you jump off? Can you find three?"
3. *Climber.* "Can you travel and then hold still, hang? Can you use different parts to grip with as you hang?" (Make it clear when you are symmetrical, asymmetrical.)
4. *Ropes.* Change between using two ropes and using one rope as you swing, climb and hang. Can you use two feet to take off with and make even shapes as you suspend and balance?

8 Years

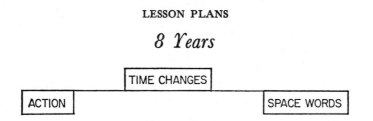

Lesson Content: 1

Exploring acceleration and deceleration within a series of actions, which may be the same or different.

FLOORWORK

Children recall different actions where they can move (*a*) QUICKLY, (*b*) SLOWLY. The response may be in terms of running, jumping, using hands and feet in different ways, or rolling.

EXPLORATION OF TIME CHANGES

1. Choose an action. Can you start SLOWLY, then get QUICKER and stop? Try this several times.
2. Choose a different action, can you ACCELERATE then SLOW DOWN?

OBSERVATION AND GUIDANCE

1. Observe the children as they are working, guide them as to the APPROPRIATENESS of their actions in relation to the task and give them help where needed.
2. Children explore the feel of running, shooting upwards and stopping. Starting from stillness, on their toes, children should feel the gradual ACCELERATION AND GATHERING OF TENSION AND ENERGY, which explodes upwards in a jump and is then contained as they land and pause. Ask the children what kind of landing is being used. Appreciation that the two-foot landing is helpful, and an awareness of the use of the legs as they thrust away from the floor, then meet the floor and absorb the body weight, is important.
3. Children explore the linking of different actions and "play" with the idea of ACCELERATING and DECELERATING.

APPARATUS WORK

Examples of group tasks.
It should be remembered that when working on this theme, apparatus

which provides length or allows for the building up of momentum, *e.g.* ropes, is helpful.

1. *Ropes.* Move with your rope, can you build up speed until you leave the floor? Choose the moment when you land, can you slow down? If space allows, explore the idea of spinning and going around, also building up speed then slowing down.
2. *Box, two mats.* Arrive on the box quickly, move along it slowly, cross a mat quickly. What different actions can you use?
3. *Bench, mat.* Running and jumping. Can you land and slow down along the mat?
4. *Bar, inclined bench, mat.* Use different actions. Can you speed up, slow down, as you travel upwards? downwards?

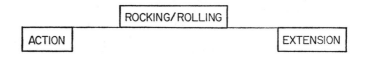

Lesson Content: 2

Specific exploration of rocking and rolling.

FLOORWORK

1. Ask the children to begin by TRAVELLING FREELY—this will involve the use of different parts of the body, *e.g.* feet, hands, surfaces.
2. After the initial burst of activity, ask the children to find different ways of moving on the BROAD SURFACES, *e.g.* BACK, SIDES, FRONT of the body. Allow time for this experimentation, and be aware that it may be necessary to step in and give guidance, *e.g.* "can you change from one surface to another?"

OBSERVATION

Select two children who may give a contrasting response—A rocking, B rolling. Ask the children "what is the difference between these two actions?" Answer: "B keeps changing from one surface to another, while A keeps going to and fro along the same surface." The children may also notice that A's spine was held in a rounded way while B's may change between rounded or straight.

EXPLORATION OF ROCKING

TRY DIFFERENT WAYS OF ROCKING. Use different STARTING POINTS, *e.g.* back surfaces, tummy. Experiment with placing of limbs, *e.g.* hands on floor to push off, gripping ankles, etc. Make it SMOOTH—NO BUMPS as your weight goes to and fro, forwards and backwards or side to side.

The children may discover that rocking is easier (*a*) when they build up momentum and size of movement and (*b*) on their back surface when the spine is curled as opposed to rocking on their tummy when the spine must arch.

ROLLING

Change from rocking to rolling—make it smooth as you keep CHANGING FROM ONE SURFACE TO ANOTHER. "Can you roll when you are curled up? stretched long and narrow?" Remember to tuck the bony parts in— elbows, knees, head.

Children may discover that whereas in rocking the surfaces of the body are naturally next to each other, in rolling the parts may be either anatomically adjacent or be brought into that situation, *e.g.* shoulders next to feet in a forward roll.

This section of work should conclude with some running and jumping where the emphasis on movement away from the floor contrasts with the previous experience and is a further preparation for work on apparatus.

APPARATUS WORK

Apparatus with flat surfaces will enable the children to make use of their previous experience, *e.g.* benches, flat beams, boxes, mats.

Examples of group tasks

1. *Springboard, mat.* Free running, jumping. Can you ROLL ALONG THE MAT ON LANDING?
2. *Two benches, two mats.* Make your own arrangement of apparatus. Travel along, on and off. Can you put in a ROCKING ACTION, a ROLLING ACTION?
3. *Inclined bench, bar, box, mat.* Use a ROCKING ACTION at some point, then show CONTRASTING ACTIONS as you travel along, on and off.
4. *Beam, mats.* Explore the idea of ROLLING AROUND THE BEAM, use the space between the beam and the mat to go through in different ways.

The work on surfaces which has developed these rocking and rolling actions could continue in the next lesson(s). The children could develop work on sliding, pushing and pulling actions where a body surface remains in constant contact with another surface. Secondly, they might develop a movement sequence containing the ideas such as jump and roll, rock then balance. The sequence could be repeated with a change in the size of the actions.

8–9 Years

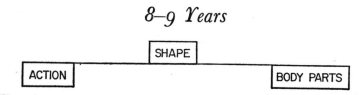

Lesson Content: 1

Body shape in motion and stillness. The exploration of the fundamental body shapes of long and narrow, broad and spread out, rounded and ball-like, screw-like and twisted.

FLOORWORK GUIDANCE

Children work in their own space, revise ways of curling, stretching, arching and twisting using different parts of the body to balance on. Questions such as "what parts of the body help you in curling? can you find different ways of twisting?" can be asked.

SHAPE EXPLORATION

1. TRAVEL IN YOUR OWN WAY. Can you make different SHAPES as you travel? Give time for the children to explore and encourage them as they experiment.
2. JUMPING. As you jump can you make a SHAPE IN THE AIR? How many different shapes can you make?
3. BALANCING. Use different parts of your body to balance on. What SHAPES can you make?

OBSERVATION

Teacher and children observe a small group in action who, between them, may have given the basic shapes. Ask the children what is the main

74

difference of each shape? Is there one shape we haven't seen? For example, screw-like may not have been observed, especially in jumping. Give the children a challenge "Can you make yourself move, wriggle in the air? Hips and shoulders going in different directions?"

GUIDANCE

1. LOCOMOTION. Use hands and feet only. Can you make these FOUR SHAPES that you have seen AS YOU TRAVEL?
2. Use the SURFACES OF THE BODY, *e.g.* spine, sides. Can you change SHAPE as you travel? This task will give the characteristic actions of rolling, but children can discover that they can be ball-like or elongated as they roll or even momentarily broad and spread out.

APPARATUS WORK

Examples of group tasks.

Because the children are dealing with a new movement idea, much of the work will be largely experimental, the clarification and formulation of phrases of movement developing in succeeding lessons.

1. *Bench, mat.* Use hands and feet as you travel—what SHAPES can you make?
2. *Box, mat.* Get on in your own way. Jump off and make a CLEAR SHAPE IN THE AIR.
3. *Climber.* What SHAPES can you make as you travel up and down and through the spaces?
4. *Two bars, inclined bench, mat.* Use ONE SHAPE as you travel along the bench, can you make a DIFFERENT SHAPE as you go through the space, over the bar?

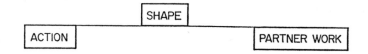

Lesson Content: 2

Body shape in motion and stillness. Further development of the children's experience of four basic shapes.

LESSON PLANS

FLOORWORK

As the children are changing, ask if they can remember what they were working on in the previous lesson.
Answer: SHAPES.

GUIDANCE

As soon as you are ready, go and begin working. Can you make these shapes in different actions?

OBSERVATION

1. Observe children working. Select one child to show one of the basic shapes. Focus children's attention on HOW this shape is ACHIEVED, then extend their experience of this shape in different actions, *e.g.* long and narrow. What parts of the body HELP US to achieve this shape? Spine, arms, fingertips, stretching into space above the head, feet stretching in opposite direction. Can you find different actions where you are long and narrow?
2. WORK THROUGH THE OTHER BASIC SHAPES, encouraging the children to find another way of moving and yet still attaining the particular shape being focussed upon, *e.g.* rounded, ball-like, achieved in jumping, rolling, crab-like actions.

FORMULATE

Work with a partner. Use the idea of moving TOWARDS, OVER and AWAY FROM your partner and develop a phrase of movement where you show three of the basic shapes in different actions. Further clarification may come in terms of "how do you begin?", "what shape do you end with in stillness?"

APPARATUS WORK

Examples of group tasks.

1. *Climber.* Can you make DIFFERENT SHAPES as you hang, climb, swing? Show two different shapes that you can make.
2. *Long mat.* Work with a partner. Can you MATCH each other's shape? CONTRAST shapes? In travelling and balance.
3. *Two benches, two mats.* Travel along one bench using hands and feet only—what shapes can you make as you travel? On the second

bench use the body surfaces—make a CLEAR SHAPE as you travel then CHANGE SHAPE along the mat.

4. *Box, mat.* Find your own way of getting on. Can you MATCH your partner's shape in the air? As you travel along the mat?

9 Years

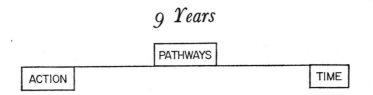

Lesson Content

The discovery that movement can be planned to follow a clearly defined pathway. The use of straight, angular and curving pathways.

FLOORWORK AND EXPLORATION OF PATHWAYS

1. Travel freely on your feet, *e.g.* running, jumping, skipping. If you HAD PAINT ON YOUR FEET, WHAT KIND OF PATHWAY WOULD THEY TRACE ON THE FLOOR? Show me. Can you trace a different pathway? —and another?

2. Allow time for this experimentation before REINFORCING what the children are doing by a brief period of observation, *e.g.* a small group may, between them, show pathways which are curving and angular. Do they know the difference between an angular pathway and a curved pathway?

3. Ask the children to use different actions TO BRING ABOUT A CHANGE OF LEVEL as they continue to experiment with the idea of tracing a floor pathway using straight lines, curves.

FORMULATE

Ask the children to invent a movement sequence which traces a floor pattern—make the beginning and ending clear.

OBSERVATION

1. Half the class working, watched by the other half. Ask the observers if they can pick out any SPECIFIC PATHWAYS WHICH MAY SUGGEST A PARTICULAR SHAPE, *e.g.* a CIRCLE, SQUARE.

2. The children now clarify their own track or they may try out a new one inspired, perhaps, by their period of observation.

CLASS ACTIVITY

Half the class working with benches, the other half working with mats and hoops.

GUIDANCE

1. *Benches.* Use different actions and MAKE ANGULAR PATHWAYS as you travel along or on and off the benches.
2. *Mat, hoop placed on the floor.* Explore the idea of MAKING A CURVED PATHWAY GOING AROUND THE HOOP (the hoop acting as a focal point), CROSSING THE HOOP AND MAT USING A STRAIGHT PATHWAY.

After allowing time for experimentation, one could draw attention to the Time factor, *e.g.* "are they travelling along their pathway quickly? slowly?—make it clear!" One could also draw on any previous material that is familiar to the children to spark off further creativity in relation to this theme.

In many schools, the time allowed for a movement period is often all too short and the class activity may be the climax of this particular lesson, any further development of the children's ideas taking place on major apparatus in the succeeding lesson or lessons.

9—10 Years

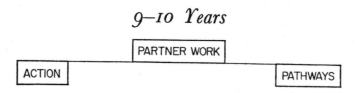

Lesson Content

Partner work using the idea of a facing situation linked with working along a straight pathway. It is assumed that the children have already had some experience of partner work.

FLOORWORK AND GUIDANCE

Individual practice of different actions travelling along a straight line and returning back along the same track. Give verbal cues if necessary which draw upon the children's previous experience, *e.g.* change of level, change of shape or the speed of actions.

PARTNER WORK PROBLEM

1. Find a partner. Start facing each other but some distance away. PROBLEM: HOW ARE THEY TO EXCHANGE PLACES AND YET MOVE ALONG A STRAIGHT PATHWAY? Some children might solve the problem by going over or under their partner with or without contact, others might step or "squeeze" round each other!

2. To develop this idea further, ask the children to find a way of RETURNING TO THEIR STARTING POINT. Some children might respond by returning back along the same track, others might establish a second track by curving or zig-zagging back to their starting point.

APPARATUS WORK

Examples of group tasks.

1. *Horse, bench, two mats.* Make your own arrangement of apparatus. At some point WORK TOWARDS YOUR PARTNER ON A STRAIGHT PATHWAY.

2. *Two boxes placed lengthways to each other with a space between, mats placed at the sides of both boxes.* Start facing each other and TRAVEL UNTIL YOU HAVE EXCHANGED PLACES, return to your starting point ALONG A STRAIGHT PATHWAY.

3. *One large-sized hoop.* A holds the hoop and MOVES WITH IT ALONG A STRAIGHT PATHWAY, perhaps changing the angle at which it is held, while B MOVES IN AND OUT of the hoop.

4. *Climbing frame, bench, mat.* Work with a partner. At some point can you FOLLOW ALONG THE SAME TRACK?

As stated in Chapter V, some apparatus work where the children have a choice as to whether they pursue their own ideas or work with a partner should be included.

10–11 Years

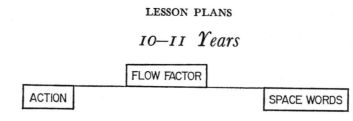

Lesson Content

Guided experience of the Flow Factor.

FLOORWORK

The children to begin by travelling freely, using all the space. Ask the children to move HIGH then LOW, AWAY from the floor then CLOSE to it.

GUIDANCE AND FREE FLOW

Action ideas: leaping, turning, rolling, spinning. Ask the children to keep MOVING CONTINUOUSLY, SMOOTHLY. Let one action MELT INTO ANOTHER —go High then Low, use all the space—and rest.

BOUND FLOW

1. Work in your own space. "Hold a balanced position, now CARE- FULLY CHANGE TO ANOTHER POSITION—GRIP TIGHT, STILL; CHANGE AGAIN AND CHECK. Are you on-balance?"
2. Use STEP-LIKE actions—be ready to put in a STOP at any moment, *e.g.* on a signal.
3. Include SURFACES for actions such as rolling, sliding. Again stress the feel for CAREFUL PLACEMENT of the body and the READINESS TO STOP.

   Ask the children "what is the DIFFERENCE IN FEELING between these two experiences?" The answers should relate to the feeling of flow in movement, *i.e.* continuous, on-going, streaming-free flow or careful, ready to stop, tight-bound flow. Recapitulate in movement the feel of these two qualities before beginning work on apparatus.

APPARATUS WORK

Examples of group tasks.

1. *Ropes.* Use ideas of spinning, turning and running with your rope(s) before gripping and stopping on the rope(s).
2. *Two bars, mats.* How smoothly, continuously can you move through,

over, under and around the bars. Can you use turns, spins to help the feel of free flow?

Or balance on one bar then carefully move down on to the mat or up high to the bar above and balance again.

3. *Danish bar, bench, mat.* Travel as High as you can along the bar, can you put in a balance? Use the bench to travel non-stop in different ways then land and balance on the mat.

4. *Two inclined benches, two mats.* The benches could be inclined against a climber or a stool. Find different ways of travelling up and down the benches. Make it clear when you are stressing continuity—going—or checking and careful placement.

The Progression of Work

While it is difficult to programme a scheme of work, since the needs of individual classes and age groups will differ one from another according to previous experience, environmental conditions and so on, there should be an appreciation of the need for some kind of "ordering" of the children's movement experience.

The movement chart in Figure 11, showing the progressive development of movement material over a span of five years, was designed to assist in planning a scheme of work which reflected the "wholeness" of movement, while drawing attention to themes within the four major areas. The themes felt to be most relevant to the different stages of development are shown in heavy type; sub-themes may be selected from the children's previous experience either from adjoining areas within the same circle or from a previous year's work. For example, when taking Partner Work for the first time with seven–eight-year-olds, a sub-theme of Levels could be taken from within the same circle. Alternatively, a sub-theme of Time could be taken, which is a recapitulation of work done in the previous year.

All the movement material can be returned to at different stages and be further developed and refined. This can be very rewarding both for the children and the teacher, since it taxes movement memory, provides for a deepening of movement understanding and can enable the children to perceive not only relationships within the theme but with other movement ideas.

What should clearly emerge as a result of these interlocking experiences is not the contrived and the stereotyped, but a child with a movement response which reveals a wide vocabulary of action, who is articulate in the use of the body in space, sensitive and rhythmically aware and has a growing ability to work with a partner in a variety of ways.

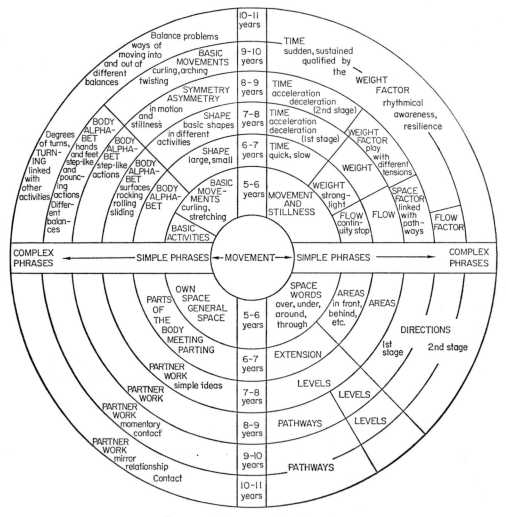

Fig. 11.—The progression of work.

CHAPTER X

Gymnastics and Competition

Introduction

THE question of competition is one which has come increasingly to the fore within the last decade and, in view of recent developments such as the British Amateur Gymnastics Award scheme, the national schools junior team and the growing popularity of Olympic gymnastics as a sport form, is one which should be considered by all teachers of this age range. While I believe that each approach to gymnastic work has something to contribute to the other, the mixing of ballet technique with set gymnastic skills, which has caused one critic to take the view that Olympic gymnastics is 'ballet without art!'[1] should cause all concerned with gymnastic education to re-appraise the direction which the Olympic form of gymnastics is taking.

Perhaps the initiators of the B.A.G.A. scheme, aimed initially at secondary schools but now being directed towards younger children, should be congratulated on capitalising on the known acquisitiveness of young children for collecting things! Its protagonists claim that "our P.E. system doesn't teach its skills" and that this scheme is the best way of beginning.[2] While it may be true that stereotyped closed skills are not the basis of an educational gymnastics lesson, skilful movement arises from work which is more open-ended, which nevertheless enables children to capture the characteristic actions of gymnastics with greater possibility of developing variations through the understanding of movement concepts. Through a movement approach, the children's learning becomes their own.

For the potential Olga Korbuts of this world, with their predisposition to a particular physique and temperament, it may well be that this scheme has value. Indeed, judging from the initial impact of the B.A.G.A. awards there is con-clusive evidence that for some children they fulfil a need and may well prove a powerful motivator. The dangers lie in the exaggerated hyper-extension required in certain movements which may ultimately prove harmful to the spine and in the possibility that for the teacher with little time for lesson preparation, the scheme may become an easy way out. On carefully selected occasions it should be recognised that they provide one means of measuring progress, albeit in arbitrary fashion.

It is not always appreciated that educational gymnastics can be placed within the context of competition and be assessed. Just as a choir, an athletics team or a drama group may participate in competitions and festivals so may this form of participation prove a worthwhile extension of work for children at the top end of the primary school and into the secondary school, the main criteria for assessment being the degree of inventiveness, appropriateness and mastery shown by the children.

When considering the question of inventiveness, there should be concern for the degree of originality which is revealed by a child's ability to make new combinations of movements whether in floorwork or on the apparatus. The appropriateness of these ideas in relation to the stated theme is an important factor, and here there should be avoidance of movement which is sheer novelty, gimmicky and unrelated to a movement sequence. On the other hand, there should be concern for the avoidance of movement clichés. Finally, were the children able to appreciate the scope of their own ideas and perfect them? Was there a sense of poise and finish to their work?

Preparation

Many teachers will already be familiar with the kind of thinking and pre-planning which is a vital element of successful competitions. The following points are suggestions for those who may be unfamiliar with the necessary planning.

I. FOR THE CHILDREN

1. Inform them in good time of the nature of the meeting (suggested time, six weeks). Advertise the day, date and timing.
2. Discuss with the children the movement themes and be clear in defining and distinguishing set work from free choice activity.
3. Give children ample opportunity for working out their ideas and appreciating the span of time that they will have in which to present their work on the day.
4. Provide for extra practice times when the children can work at their ideas and perfect them. This may require a rota system for the use of the work space during the lunch hour and or after

school—there may even be the need to enlist the help of colleagues to help with the supervision.

2. ADJUDICATION

1. If drawn from outside the school, invite the judges in good time and give them a clear idea of what is involved, the time schedule and the groups to be assessed.

2. Generally it is better that there is adjudication with comments for each group of children and a summary of the work as a whole rather than precise marking. If marks are to be awarded make sure the basis of this is understood. Specific guidance on the allocation of marks can be gained from reference to the International Gymnastic Federation rule book *Code of Points*.

3. Prepare adjudication sheets for each group to be assessed with relevant headings, for example:

CLASS ....   THEME ....

	Bodily awareness and inventiveness	Development of ideas, continuity	Unity and quality of performance
FLOORWORK 1. Set work 2. Free choice			
APPARATUS 1. Set ...... 2. Set ...... 3. Free choice 4.			

SPECIAL COMMENTS :

_____
_____
_____

Further points which are helpful to such an occasion are:

1. Special seating arrangements for participants and spectators.
2. The use of older children to act as stewards.
3. The provision of programmes and scoreboards, the latter necessary if marks are to be awarded.

85

For those children with *special talents* in this form of movement, such experience can prove a further challenge to their skill and serve as a transition stage to later participation in Olympic gymnastics. It should never be forgotten, however, that children need to enjoy gymnastic activity for its own sake and at *their own level*. Teachers should be aware of the dangers of pressurising children into competition simply to satisfy the needs of national or local bodies for sporting prestige, however persuasive the publicity campaigns may be.

REFERENCES

1. R. Buckle, Review in the *Sunday Times*, 13.5.1973.
2. Mrs. P. Prestidge in an article by S. Levenson, *The Times Educational Supplement*, 17.9.1971.

CHAPTER XI

The Relationship of Gymnastics with Other Studies

THE uniqueness of gymnastic work, which is a distinct form of movement activity which allows children to move in an acrobatic way as they play with gravity, is something which children have a right to enjoy for its own sake and there is a real sympathy for the child who asks "do I have to write about it?" or even "do I have to paint it?" Nevertheless, there are occasions when work experienced in one sphere can not only initiate but also reinforce work in other areas of knowledge which, in turn, may be illuminated through links with other disciplines. The appreciation of these cross-links may contribute to an ideas network which significantly enhances children's learning experiences.

Movement and speech are closely related since both are primarily physical before they become communicative. The careful and imaginative use of language by the teacher may stimulate a correspondingly articulate use of movement, thus increasing a child's control of both language and action while fostering wider powers of expression. Observation will reveal the children responding to the physical texture of words in the quality of their action, quite apart from the intellectual response that words demand. The use of flash cards may serve as visual reinforcement during the lesson or they may be placed in the classroom situation as "new words that we know."

Experiences of pattern-making in the visual arts, where circles, zig-zags and straight lines form a basis might also in gymnastics generate movement activity where the idea of formulating a sentence of action along a specific pathway is the discipline of the lesson.

From experience of symmetry and asymmetry in motion and stillness the children might gain a clearer understanding of work done on forms of symmetry in mathematics. In the visual arts, the appreciation of symmetry of form, which may give security, stability and strength of expression, could be contrasted with the greater sense of motion which asymmetry gives within a static form.

Investigating problems of balance in movement may initiate scientific

G   87

investigation into the basic principles of equilibrium in objects. Experience and mastery of changing tensions in action may lead children to a fuller comprehension of Newton's laws of motion.

In all these instances, they have also acquired a sense of their own uniqueness, a knowledge that they are capable of thinking and realising ideas in terms of action.

Lessons which demand disciplined thinking in terms of movement, yet which are enjoyable, can make a valuable contribution to children's movement education. If, in addition, there is the opportunity to further the understanding of concepts through other forms of experience, teachers can enable a child's world to become more than a collection of inert ideas, of arbitrary subject boundaries. The world begins to cohere, and children's perception of it and relationship to it steadily expands.

Bibliography

Brearley, M. *et al. Fundamentals in the First School*, Basil Blackwell, Oxford, 1969.

Brearley, M. and Hitchfield, E. *A Teacher's Guide to Reading Piaget*, Routledge and Kegan Paul, 1966.

Brown, M. and Sommer, B. *Movement Education: its evolution and a modern approach*, Addison-Wesley Publishing Company, 1969.

Cameron, W. McD. and Pleasance, Peggy. *Education in Movement: School Gymnastics*, Basil Blackwell, Oxford, 1963.

Gilliom, B. *Basic Movement Education: Rationale and Teaching Units*, Addison-Wesley Publishing Company, 1970.

Inhelder, B., Piaget, J. and Szeminska, A. *The Child's Conception of Geometry*, Routledge and Kegan Paul, 1960.

Jordan, D. *Childhood and Movement*, Basil Blackwell, Oxford, 1966.

Knapp, B. *Skill in Sport, the attainment of proficiency*, Routledge and Kegan Paul, 1963.

Koestler, A. *The Act of Creation*, Hutchinson and Company Limited, 1964.

Laban, Rudolf. *Modern Educational Dance*, 2nd Edition, third impression, Macdonald and Evans Limited, 1968.

Laban, Rudolf and Lawrence, F. C. *Effort*, Macdonald and Evans Limited, 2nd Edition, 1973.

Mauldon, E. and Layson, J. *Teaching Gymnastics*, Macdonald and Evans Limited, eighth impression 1971.

Morison, R. *A Movement Approach to Educational Gymnastics*, Dent and Sons Limited, 1969.

Mosston, M. *Teaching Physical Education*, Charles Merrill Publishing Company, 1966.

Pallet, D. G. *Modern Educational Gymnastics*, Pergamon Press, 1965.

Peters, R. S. *Education as Initiation*, George G. Harrap and Co. Ltd., London, 1964.

Piaget, J. and Inhelder, B. *The Child's Conception of Space*, Routledge and Kegan Paul, 1963.

Redfern, B. *Introducing Laban Art of Movement*, Macdonald and Evans Limited, third impression 1971.

89

BIBLIOGRAPHY

Sweeney, R. *et al. Selected Readings in Movement Education*, Addison-Wesley Publishing Company, 1970.

Streicher, M. *Reshaping Physical Education*, Manchester University Press, 1970.

Department of Education and Science, *Movement—Physical Education in the Primary School*, 1972.

Index

INDEX

K

Kinesthetic sense, 8, 18, 37, 39
Knapp, B, 49
Koestler, A., 38

L

Laban, R., 4, 29
Landing, ways of, 12, 13
Lesson planning, 58–82
  conclusion, 58
  evaluation, 54
  selection of content, 52, 53

M

Material of movement, 7–38
Memory, 37, 59, 82
Morison, R., 4
Motion factors, 20–27
  of flow, 26, 27
  of space, 25
  of time, 23, 24, 25
  of weight, 20, 21, 22
Movement approach, 4–6
Movement education, (vi), 3, 5, 6, 88
Movement ideas, 59, 84
Movement logic, 18, 27

N

Nash, J. B., 5

O

Observation, 37, 39–42, 55
  criteria, 41, 42
  observers, 40, 41
  performers, 41
  teacher's, 39
  value, 42
Obstacle, 37
Olympic gymnastics, 5, 83, 86

P

Partner work, 34–38, 68, 78, 79
  starting situations, 35
  with and without contact, 34
  value, 37, 38
Piaget, J., 29
Pouncing and springing, 12
Preparation and recovery, 11, 14
Progression of work, 81, 82

R

Relationship, working with others, 34–38, 67
Resilience, 10
Rhythm in movement, 14, 23
Rocking, rolling, 15, 72, 73

S

Space awareness, 28–33
  areas, 30, 61
  directional awareness, 31
  extension, 29, 61
  levels, 29, 63
  pathways, 31, 77
  words, 28
Speed, variations of, 23–25, 64, 71
Step-like actions, 14

T

Teaching method, 55–57
Tension, 21–23
Themes, 52, 60–81
Transference of weight, (v)

U

Ullman, L., 4

W

Williams, J. F., 5
Wording of tasks, 40, 53, 56